Does God really hate me?
Why do I feel so worthless?
What if I mess up ... again?
Is the God of the Bible really
that judgmental?

DAMN SHAME

Finding Freedom from False Beliefs

By Curtis H. Tucker

Straight Street Books
Lighthouse Publishing of the Carolinas

DAMN SHAME BY CURTIS H. TUCKER
Published by Straight Street Books, an imprint of Lighthouse Publishing of the Carolinas, 2333 Barton Oaks Dr., Raleigh, NC, 27614.

ISBN 978-1-938499-40-1
Copyright © 2016 by Curtis H. Tucker
Cover Design by: Elaina Lee
Interior design by Atritex, www.atritex.com

Available in print from your local bookstore, online, or from the publisher at: lighthousepublishingoftheCarolinas.com.

For more information on this book and the author visit: www.curtishtucker.com.

Unless otherwise stated, all Scripture quotations are taken from the New American Standard Bible®, Copyright © 1960, 1962, 1963, 1968, 1971, 1972, 1973, 1975, 1977, 1995 by The Lockman Foundation (www.Lockman.org). Used by permission.

Scripture quotations taken from the HOLY BIBLE NEW INTERNATIONAL VERSION r. NIVr Copyright © 1973, 1978, 1984 by International Bible Society. Used by permission of Zondervan Publishing House. All rights reserved.

Scripture quotations from THE MESSAGE. Copyright © by Eugene H. Peterson 1993, 1994, 1995, 1996, 2000, 2001, 2002. Used by permission of NavPress Publishing Group.

Brought to you by the creative team at Lighthouse Publishing of the Carolinas: Eddie Jones, Andrea Merrell, Cindy Sproles, Shonda Savage, and Brian Cross.

Library of Congress Cataloging-in-Publication Data
Tucker, Curtis H.
Damn Shame/ Curtis H. Tucker 1st ed.

Printed in the United States of America

Praise for *Damn Shame* ...

From a pastoral and theological perspective, *Damn Shame* addresses one of the most important problems among Christians today. This is a vital message for those who find themselves working the Christian life harder but enjoying Jesus less.

> ~ Ed Underwood, Pastor, Church of the Open Door
> Author of *When God Breaks Your Heart*,
> *Reborn to Be Wild*, and *The Trail*

This is an important work from Curtis Tucker, and I do believe it has the ability to be life-changing for many readers. As our view of God and of self becomes whole, freedom becomes a reality, and our hope for the future begins to soar. I recommend it highly.

> ~ Robert Ricciardelli, Founder, the Converging Zone
> Owner - Choose Growth

A must-read for every believer, especially for those who have had a legalistic experience that drove them to feel unworthy, or never able to be good enough or to do enough good works to matter. People who have felt unworthy, out of touch with their Creator, driven by a performance-oriented, religious culture, will find in these pages liberating information.

> ~ George Meisinger
> Chancellor, Chafer Theological Seminary

Damn Shame gave voice to many of my wrestlings and questions about why I struggle so much to truly believe my worth in the eyes of God. Could it be that He loves me—all of me—insecurities and all? Curtis Tucker gently leads readers toward a whole view of God's love and how it's beautifully lavished on us all.

> ~ Mary DeMuth, Author
> *Worth Living: How God's Wild Love for You Makes You Worthy*

When I was assigned as the editor for *Damn Shame*, I had no idea of the impact this book would have on me personally. The author's examples of people riddled with shame reminded me all too clearly of the baggage I carried around for most of my life, all because of the verbal abuse I suffered while growing up. The old adage about sticks and stones is a lie. Words are powerful, and they leave wounds that can last a lifetime. They can make us think, *If my parents don't love and value me, how can God possibly feel any different?* If you have believed the lies that shout, "You are NO GOOD and you never will be; you don't even deserve to be alive," I can assure you that *Damn Shame* will break down those walls the enemy has constructed to keep you separated from God and dispel every misconception you have ever entertained about a loving heavenly Father. I wish there had been a book like this years ago when I was desperately struggling to make sense of everything wrong in my world. Be prepared. The words in this book will change your life forever.

~ Andrea Merrell, Editor
Author of *Murder of a Manuscript* and *Praying for the Prodigal*

Dedication

This book is dedicated to all those who hide,
yet are desperate to come out of the bushes
and experience authentic, whole-hearted living
and the love of the living God.

Acknowledgements

A debt of gratitude goes out to my spiritual family
at Redmond Community Church who supports and
encourages me to dig deep in the Scriptures, ask
questions, doubt, and believe.

Also, I want to thank Kevin and Susan for the use of
their wonderful cabin on the beautiful McKenzie River
to kick off this writing project.

Thanks to David and Sarah Van Diest for the constant
encouragement to write and, especially, Sarah's
consummate partnership on this manuscript.

Table of Contents

Foreword

Over the years and around the world, I've sat in stadiums full of thousands of tennis fans to watch players I had coached compete on the highest stages of the game. In time, I developed what many call a "professional eye." Though I saw the same match unfold as the crowd of fans, we observed two totally different sides of the game. My eyes had learned to see beyond what most could see.

Jesus often told His listeners that to understand what He was truly saying they would need "eyes to see and ears to hear." The eyes and ears found on our heads are not the only eyes and ears we come equipped with. These natural eyes are lenses that feed us visual information, and the ears are funnels that help us hear the noise around us. But it is a different set of eyes and ears our Lord was talking about. This second set works on a spiritual level.

Deep within our beings, where these eyes and ears reside, we find eternal life and our true identity. Instead of natural lenses taking in information, these eyes are projectors, projecting the truth that is present within any given moment of our lives. Here we also find a new set of ears that, instead of helping us hear the noise of this world, enable us to listen to the truth behind our experiences.

In *Damn Shame*, Curtis Tucker brings focus to a spiritual issue we've tried to understand with our natural senses. Changing which set of eyes and ears we use—from the natural to the spiritual—enables us to grasp the underlying truth about shame, but also about God, ourselves, and who we are to Him. This new perspective is where the force of truth breaks way to freedom.

Today, your life is either being led by truth or driven by a need to cover up shame. It is very possible that as you read, you will find all your efforts—professional, personal, and spiritual—have failed to deliver happiness and peace because they have all been powered by shame. Do not despair and don't panic. This does not have to be the end of the story.

I encourage you to read this book slowly. Allow the pearls of wisdom and truth to awaken your heart and your ability to see and hear with that second set of eyes and ears. Let His grace penetrate the brokenness of your inner world where His love can heal you, so you are able to love, see, and hear with the whole of your heart.

Yes, shame is powerful, but the love and grace of the King are greater and more than able to help you drop the fig leaf of shame that has been covering all that is good and true about God, life, and your true self.

Travel well, aware and free, my friend!

~ Pablo Giacopelli
Author of *Holding on Loosely* and *The Modern Fig Leaf*

Chapter 1-ish
Two Rivers

The best way out is always through.[1]
~ Robert Frost

In Central Oregon where I live, there is a favorite playground for outdoor enthusiasts called Lake Billy Chinook. The lake has a surface area of 3,997 acres (or forty-six miles) and a max depth of 415 feet. It's fed by three rivers: Crooked River, Deschutes River, and Metolius River. Each river is unique in and of itself, yet the purest of the three, with pristine, aqua-blue water, is the Metolius. The twenty-nine miles of this gorgeous river has its beginnings in two clusters of springs near the base of Black Butte. The water flow is as consistent as its 48-degree Fahrenheit temperature. While all three rivers brim with life and are similarly beautiful, the Metolius stands distinct in its purity and beauty.

All three flow into one body of water and become indistinguishable one from another. The outflow of the three is reduced to one on the other side of Round Butte Dam: the Deschutes River. Not taking anything away from the Crooked or Deschutes rivers, both are beautiful, but both are much warmer than the Metolius. So while they are wonderful to look at, they are more susceptible to contaminants and algae, which cause them to be a deeper greenish-blue. The distinctiveness and pristine beauty of the Metolius is lost in the merging of the three rivers.

God's universal love for all humanity is like this beautiful and unique river: pure, pristine, and constant. Yet God's love is lost as it merges with another river, the river of shame. Shame is like a river that tends to override the purity of God's unconditional and universal love. Shame speaks so loudly and so persistently that God's message of worth and significance for every single human being gets lost in the vastness of a turbulent current of lies.

Jesus confronted the existence of two rivers in the life of the woman He met at a well (John 4:1-42).

When Jesus spoke with the Samaritan woman at the well, He knew fully that the purity of God's pristine love in her life had been consumed by a river of shame. That river had filled her like a lake and drowned out the river of the life of God. She may not have ever considered the headwaters of her shame, but she knew she was *less than*. She was a Samaritan.

She asked Jesus, "How is it that you, being a Jew, ask me for a drink since I am a Samaritan woman?" (John 4:9). John adds the editorial comment in parentheses: "For Jews have no dealings with Samaritans." She lived her whole life under the lie that God did not take to her kind. She may have blamed her parents who bore her into this "half-breed" race of insignificance. She could have blamed the Jews who thought they were the only superior choice of God, consequently making her inferior and treating her accordingly. Bottom line: she had been dealt a bad hand and considered herself unworthy and unlovable. And she was not alone.

The disciples, the ones who had been with Jesus, reveal another angle of shame that was at work in their day when we read, "They were amazed that He had been speaking with a woman" (John 4:27). Apparently, living in a male dominant society—a culture in which men are better and more worthy—was another mark of shame. She was a Samaritan, and she was a woman. And if that was not enough, this woman was a floozy. Married five times and now living with a man who was not her husband (John 4:17-18), she was not measuring up. It is no surprise that she was a bit shocked when Jesus asked her for a drink.

- She was a Samaritan.
- She was a woman.
- She knew it ... as did everyone else.
- She was a promiscuous woman ... a real sinner by the standard of her day.
- She lived in darkness.
- Shame had completely drowned out the purity of a loving God.

A sociologist or psychologist could have come alongside the woman at the well and offered her some helpful insights as to why her behavior and decisions pointed to a deeper issue of shame. They may have been able to offer some insights as to why she experienced shame or why her parents used those harmful techniques to raise her. Those experts may have offered some valid exercises to help the woman move away from the shame to more wholehearted living. But how long would it last? How sure could she ever be on the word of another human being, albeit one with credentials? How convinced would anybody be?

If you want to deal with the source of all shame, you have to dam up the river of the lie and open the floodgates of the river of life—the truth about who God is and how He sees every human being. He is our Creator, so His word should carry more weight. Sociological and psychological studies and assistance can be very helpful, but until we deal with the issue of shame at the divine level, we are only skimming the surface and have yet to unleash the river of life that overflows and leaves our thirst for significance completely quenched.

The Samaritan woman's shame was sourced in the headwaters of a lie: God is erratic, selective, and determines worth on the basis of external factors such as origin, upbringing, gender, and performance. No doubt her parents fostered the lie by teaching her she was not as significant as others, even if they were oblivious to the source of their own shame and shaming. Others in her society reinforced the message by isolating her kind, avoiding and looking down on her. But all roads—or rivers for this matter—trace back to the headwaters of shame, a lie that God is as Satan has made Him out to be.

In contrast, Jesus said there is another river available that is able to not only fill you but to overflow. That river is the river of life—the life of God, as He truly is. He loves all and considers all worthy of His love. God does not pick and choose randomly, nor on the basis of performance, origin, or gender. This is the God who "had to go through Samaria" in a day when a Jew would walk miles to avoid it. This is a God who seeks such people to be His worshipers (John 4:23). This is a God who knows that while salvation is *from* the Jews (John 4:22), it is and always has been *for* everyone. This is a God to whom everyone matters.

And guess what? She got the message. As a result, so did many others. The story ends with a very clear indication that the river of shame had been dammed up, and the river of life was flowing ... in Samaria no less. We read, "From that city many of the Samaritans believed in Him because of the word of the woman who testified" (John 4:39).

That is what happens when shame is silenced and life flows. It spills onto others.

Modern research can help us greatly by identifying patterns of behavior that are indicators of the deeper problem of shame, but lack a true solution to the source issue. We can tell people they are significant because they are unique human beings, and they are, but deep down, we long for a louder voice to cling to in times of despair: a voice that penetrates deep down and dispels lies; a voice of absolute purity in which we can have confidence. That voice is the voice of our Creator, the one who made us, the one who is Truth.

His every Word is truth (John 17:17). His Word is able to save souls (James 1:21). And when He speaks His Word to us, and we take it in, it penetrates deeply because it is "living and active and sharper than any two-edged sword, and piercing as far as the division of the soul and spirit, of both joints and marrow, and able to judge the thoughts and intentions of the heart" (Hebrews 4:12). Those deeper places are important places—places that matter to our health and well-being.

No matter how long and accurate sociological or psychological research is, it cannot even begin to match the soul-affecting, heart-healing Word of God, because God's Words are God's thoughts (Isaiah 55:8-11). And He says we are significant, each and every one of us: sinners, Samaritans, men, women, children, red, yellow, black, and white; we are precious in His sight. This is what our soul longs for ... thirsts for.

My Journey Down Two Rivers

Growing up was tough. It is for most of us. I point no fingers of blame for the shame I embraced. The people in my story had the best of intentions, even if their impact was something different. I know the same cannot be said for everyone's story. Regardless, my early childhood experiences excavated a deep groove of shame into my prefrontal cortex … and my heart. Those indelible marks became the impetus for reckless and sometimes dangerous patterns of behavior that left me unfulfilled, unhappy, and even more deeply entrenched in shame.

Worst of all, this led to living a life based in fear, concealing who I was, because revealing the true me would certainly be a disappointment. In fact, every time I did show up, which most often came out in rebellion, the message was loud and clear: WORTHLESS. Life seemingly unfolded for me in two options.

One option was to be apathetic and throw caution to the wind: *I am no good, so what's the point?* The other option was to vigorously pursue approval: *I'll show you … and everyone!* I tested both options. Even when I tried hard, gained success, and met milestones, the sense of value found in the accompanying accolades was short-lived, because that value was always tied to what lay ahead and what mountains I still hadn't conquered. But as Solomon found—and so did I—everything is vanity and chasing after the wind (Ecclesiastes 2:11). Both options ended in the same dead-end of nothingness.

Nothingness was not a good place for me. It left me despairing, although I would never let anyone know it. Henri Nouwen captures how I felt in his words, "Despair is our inner conviction that, in the end, it is utterly impossible to prevent anything from coming to nothing."[2] Everything was coming to nothing.

The sweet irony is that this *nothingness* led me to *everything*.

There wasn't a moment in time, a great awakening, or lightning bolt epiphany, but there was a definite beginning. My journey of moving beyond the nothingness of shame began at nineteen when I came to know Jesus Christ. What broke down the first walls? A message of value and worth. Someone told me God loved me and wanted to give me new life. I was empty, except for the shame that threatened to consume me, and this seemed to address my greatest and deepest immediate need. *I was in!*

After a couple of years fumbling and bumbling around a spiritual nowhere-land, I began to get with the program. While a whole new world was opening up to me, I was a far cry from being free from living a life driven by shame. The package deal of Christianity, as it was taught to me, simply replaced all the other avenues of approval seeking. I studied, prayed, served, and shared door-to-door, hoping I would gain a greater sense of approval and acceptance, or at a minimum, maintain what semblance I already had. The desire to feel valuable and worthy to God and others was insatiable. One huge mistake I made was thinking God was going to speak worth through my fellow comrades in Christianity who, unbeknownst to me, were also driven by fear and shame, looking for significance and worth. It started to feel more like a Christian competition, not a community. This left me feeling alone and disappointed.

I thought I had completely committed to a journey down the river of life, but I was still stuck in the river of shame, which I was finding had many tributaries. The scenery had changed, but it was the same water. I was adrift, lost at sea, and up the proverbial creek without a paddle.

In a culture where knowledge is king, I applied myself with all the intensity of a person on the hunt for significance by studying and pursuing knowledge. But the information I was learning, albeit good and religious, was not helping. In fact, it only made things worse. I became more and more psychologically certain that my performance in Christianity was necessary to know where I stood with God. I was taught—and accepted it almost blindly—that God had not chosen to save everyone and send all of us to heaven, and the only way I could know I was one of His chosen was to persevere in the performance of good works.

This line of thinking was right up my alley. I had grown up with the same message: *you're good only if you do good.*

So off I went doing religious good works. The harder I worked, the more tired and desperate I became. I mean, really ... how long can you go without knowing for sure that you are worthy? No matter how much I did, I never felt confident I did enough, or that the good I did was actually good enough. I soon found I was not alone. All around me were Christians desperate and depleted from the same kind of flimsy, fickle Christianity. They were driven by fear, which stemmed from their perception of an erratic God. Some, like me, were continuing to hang on by a thread, but many were dropping like flies, leaving the church, abandoning their faith, or looking for exit strategies. The pain and suffering in my own life were hard enough, but then to deal with it so consistently in the lives of others was becoming too much to handle.

What I was learning was not helping. The more I studied and learned, the more troubled I became. The more good I did, and the more proficient I got at appearances, the emptier I felt. I was experiencing worthlessness, but was unwilling or incapable of admitting it, so I masked over it all by sounding well-versed, confident, and dogmatic— despite the fact I was anything *but*. I taught the teachings that were taught to me without questioning the tenets of those truths.

Until ...

It's as though all that nothingness came in handy again. God used a dissatisfaction and desperation to open my mind and heart in order to draw me in and move me forward.

After a few years in full-time ministry, I had wrestled with the frustration and futility long enough. I became profoundly dissatisfied with the disharmony between my theology and the character of God revealed in the Bible and in the person of Jesus Christ. I grew weary of offering empty excuses like: *We will never understand these mysteries, for His thoughts are not our thoughts.* I began to seriously doubt and question traditional doctrines and teachings.

For the first time, I was fed up enough to be honest about my doubts, and in that honesty I found freedom. This newfound freedom invited me to question where I had not dared question before. Energized and encouraged, I began an honest study of the Bible that would ultimately lead me down a new path to a new option.

The lights started coming on. The Bible went from black and white to full cinematic color. And the outlandish, peculiar, and graceless teachings began to crumble and disintegrate. Suddenly, rational and reasonable options were now becoming apparent for interpreting problem passages that I had long misunderstood and misused. I no longer needed to regurgitate what others said. For so long I had sheepishly *agreed* with these flawed teachings and, at the same time, shelved them because looking directly at them was too much to deal with. Things were different. Now I had a paradigm to understand the Bible, and things were beginning to click.

This paradigm shift erased the need to give excuses to disharmonious and disgraceful teachings because now I had sensible, alternative answers—answers that harmonized with the God revealed in the Bible, especially in Jesus. This is when I realized, deeply and profoundly, as if my own personal town crier had finally been given freedom to proclaim Truth at the top of his lungs to my troubled and weary soul: *EVERY* person belongs to God, and God sees invaluable, intrinsic worth in every human soul!

And in this understanding—that every person is of worth to God— is where my soul's deliverance from shame found its running shoes. The journey began when I found Christ, and though this deliverance isn't perfect or complete, at least it's happening. This is the time when I found solace in being honest about who I am, struggles and all. This is the occasion when I first experienced what it is like to live free from the performance-driven, fear-based, fickle, Christian life I had known. And some great things have happened:

- As a man, I understand that God sees value in me independent of my performance.
- As a man, I understand that God created me uniquely, and He does not compare me to others or favor one person over another.
- As a man, I understand that I am not defined by the sum total of my weaknesses, shortcomings ... or my sins.
- As a pastor, I find surprises of grace around every corner when people who are disgruntled, disturbed, and disillusioned begin to see God in the light of who He really is.
- As a pastor, I find freedom from finding my own worth in how many butts are in the pews, how big the building and budget are, or how many missionaries we are supporting.
- Instead of ducking and dodging conversations and disagreements, I am now excited to have conversations about the truths of God's universal love and grace.
- Instead of avoiding the skeptics, I find new joy in embracing

them and joining them on their journey … and watching their
eyes light with the hope that God is, in fact, good—all the time!

I am excited about other great discoveries that are inviting me
onward, and the growth that awaits. The Bible, read as it was written,
casting off the theologies of man, continues to breathe life into my
relationship with Him, ridding me of my shame bit by bit, and others
are finding the same.

Let's join together for a journey to uncover a God who loves. A God
who accepts. A God who sees worth in you—and *every* human being.

Walk with me as we seek to rediscover a God who despises shame.

Journey with me as we identify both rivers and, hopefully, lead
many to get quenched in the river of life.

---

1 Robert Frost, *A Servant to Servants* (1914).

2 Henri Nouwen (2009-10-13). *Letters to Marc About Jesus* (Kindle Locations 198-199).
(HarperCollins, Kindle Edition).

Chapter 1
The Fire Rages

Shame is a soul eating emotion.[3]
~ Carl Jung

Mike is grown now, but to hear him tell his story, it's obvious that shame left its mark. He gets along pretty well these days, but it has not always been so easy. When he was a boy, struggling to find his way in life, he heard some crippling words from someone he deeply loved. Thirty years removed, he still remembers the exact words he heard from his father: "I can't believe my sperm could produce something as *sh!#tty* as you."

Devastating.

At that moment, the words did not sink in, but over time, they rooted down deep and festered. Those words, and the consequent feelings of shame, derailed and disrupted him for many years to come. Festering was the subconscious, and oftentimes conscious but confusing, destructive feeling of being unworthy of love, diminished, flawed, and just plain worthless. What brings a person, a parent no less, to say something so devastating and shameful? Where does that kind of stuff originate? It certainly came from somewhere.

The only reason Mike was living with his dad in the first place was because his stepfather no longer wanted him in his home. The message was not *No Vacancies*, but *Unwanted*. All he wanted was to disappear. Fueled by intense feelings of worthlessness and shame, he ran full steam into an endless cycle of empty pursuits: meaningless relationships with women, seeking to find a sense of worth and value, striving for success in sports, and tireless efforts jockeying to be in the "in" crowd. When those pursuits, among others, did not work to resolve the pain and emptiness, it was off to work in order to achieve and attain success—in order to prove his father wrong. Yet every time he heard the words "No," or "You can't do that," all he really heard was,

"You are not good enough," or more plainly, "You are no good!" This track, like every other worldly track, ended in complete emptiness. No matter where he went, he was *still there*—still existing, still standing on a square foot of soil he didn't deserve to occupy, and still breathing air that might better fill someone else's more deserving and worthy lungs.

It seems to end this way far too often.

The self-talk never changed. He was never good enough, always unlovable and unworthy. He never possessed the confidence to believe people would choose to accept him, let alone love him, for who he was. And what began as a little seed, festered and grew, affecting every other meaningful and significant relationship in his life, even his relationship with God. Mike could not imagine how God could be any different than his disappointing experiences in human relationships. If he lived an anxiety-riddled existence thinking he was damaged goods, not being sure people would choose to love him, only accepting him when or if he performed well, he naturally projected those same ideas and fears onto God.

In Mike's mind, a decision always hung in the balance, and the decision in his case was most likely: *No! You are unacceptable. You are not worthy ... not chosen. You are not good enough.* No matter what others said to try to help, he could not distance himself from the painful memories and devastating messages, nor could he see the disconnect between temporal and eternal. He did not learn until much later how unfair it was to project onto God what he had learned from other hurt and damaged souls.

That is a true-life shame story.

Shame is a devastatingly destructive force. As author Brennan Manning wrote, shame is "an invisible dragon."[4] Manning very descriptively described this beast when he wrote about shame in his memoirs: "This monster wasn't at the door big and bad; it was inside, subtle and devouring."[5]

Shame: a *monster*. How fitting.

A monster that is subtle. Internal. Devouring.

And in the words of a devoted researcher on the topic: "Shame is an epidemic."[6] That sounds pretty serious. An epidemic? *Epidemic* is

---

defined as: *affecting many individuals throughout an area at the same time; widely prevalent.*[7]

Shame an epidemic? Apparently it is, according to the expert.[8]

This worldwide epidemic of shame has been plaguing humanity and ruining lives longer and more consistently than any other known disease or outbreak. It is an epidemic more destructive than the bubonic plague. It is an epidemic that has been going on for the entirety of human history. It is an epidemic that is no respecter of persons and has no geographical boundaries or religion. This epidemic is visceral, not viral. It is a true killer.

What exactly is shame? Philosopher Bernard Williams said:

> In the experience of shame, one's whole being seems diminished or lessened. The expression of shame is not just the desire to hide, or to hide my face, but the desire to disappear, not to be there. It is not even the wish, as people say, to sink through the floor, but rather the wish that the space occupied by me should be instantaneously empty.[9]

As Brené Brown found from her years of research, "Shame is the intensely painful feeling or experience of believing that we are flawed and therefore unworthy of love and belonging."[10]

Believing I am flawed. Believing I am unworthy of love and belonging. That is the essence of shame.

Painful. Yet painfully true.

Our shame itself will not run or hide, so we feel we must disappear. We feel that the terra firma we occupy should be completely and utterly void of our existence.

Snapshots of Shame

We've all seen the face of shame. It has a particular look, though it disguises itself well.

It always hides right behind the eyes, but eventually the eyes don't lie.

I have counseled many people over the years who have struggled with this destructive force. For years, Kala carried the emotional baggage of shame after hearing her mother say, "I did not want another baby. You were a mistake." Kala's baggage was jam-packed full of thoughts and memories that left her feeling fatally flawed and wrong for existing. So destructive was this emotional luggage that she lost all confidence in herself and any hope for the future. She, too, felt like the space she occupied on this planet was underserved. Devalued and numb, her only relief from the painful emotions was by cutting herself, just to feel something. She felt like a mistake.

This is how crippling shame can be. Why would Kala's mom shame her that way? Why create such a feeling of tenuousness and lack of value? Was Kala's mom scarred by shame? Where did it all begin?

And then there was Denise, who could not escape—and has yet to recover completely from—the effects of shame. Years of abuse from a controlling and demeaning spouse left her feeling most aptly defined by the word *wrong*. How long can a person hear "You are no good!" before they actually start believing it? Denise, now far removed from that relationship, can't even go on a job interview and communicate with confidence about why the company should hire her (and it is not for lack of skill). I notice that when she speaks about herself, she shakes. Shame is a serious problem.

That is just the tip of the iceberg of the devastating effects of shame. Why, where, and when was shame awakened as a monster in this family?

And what about Brandon's story? Brandon grew up with the feeling that he could never meet the expectations put on him. It was only when the expectations were met that love was offered. If not, then love—along with his favorite toy or privilege—was taken away or withheld. Those deeply engrained messages still haunt him to this day. And those messages pop up in the strangest places and times. Recently, I spoke with Brandon. "Yesterday was a rough one," he said. When I asked him what happened, his response was, "Things were going along so good ... but then I felt oppressed by the idea that I don't deserve the good because I am not worthy."

Not worthy of good? The message runs deep: *You are no good and don't deserve good.* When things are going well, he nervously waits for the other shoe to drop and the good to come to an end. For Brandon, like many others, essential or intrinsic worth does not exist, love is conditional (or questionable), and performance earns. Bottom line: love is a decision based on a reality he has no control over and can easily be disqualified from if he doesn't perform up to par. Fortunately for Brandon, his eyes are opening to the truth, and life is changing for the better.

The same can't be said for another man I knew.

A deep sadness comes over me when I remember Joe's story. Joe was divorced, with two beautiful young daughters who were happy, joyful, and full of life. To know them was to love them. Joe was financially stable, physically healthy, well kept, owned a nice home, and was loved by his daughters, friends, and church. But something in his past was destroying him—eating him alive. One day, that feeling of wanting to disappear won out. That day, Joe took his own life, leaving his two lovely, heartbroken girls behind. Somewhere, somehow—who knows exactly when?—shame dealt a deathblow to Joe, which he carried around until it fully engulfed him, and he hid … completely. Shame kills.

Shame makes me mad. Shame makes me ask questions. Where did it come from? Where did it originate? Why is it here destroying so many lives?

These are just a few stories of how shame can impact us. Stories where somehow, someway, at some point in time, people learned devastating messages that they are damaged goods and lack intrinsic worth. They believe love is conditional; it is a choice or decision to be made with all kinds of contingencies and conditions. I know every reader could write their own story about how shame has touched, bruised, and burned them, or buried someone they loved.

It's part of our fallen state. And like in Joe's case, we don't always know what someone is dealing with because shame disguises itself or rears its ugly head in different ways based on a person's situation and personality. An outgoing temperament may show shame by lashing out in anger or control while an introverted temperament may withdraw and hide. Some people disguise shame through perfectionism or performance. Still others, by being aloof and superior. It is a mixed bag.

Here is how Brené Brown describes her own mixed bag:

> Over time I tried everything from "the good girl" with my "perform-perfect-please" routine, to clove-smoking poet, angry activist, corporate climber, and out-of-control party girl.[11]

Brown describes these not as healthy stages of developments, but as "different suits of armor" that kept her safe and distanced from people. And if those were not enough, she threw on the final coping mechanism: "always have an exit strategy."

What drives this mixed bag of reactions? Shame!

The Core

At our core, we long for relationship, acceptance, and love. Brown writes, "We are hardwired to connect with others; it's what gives purpose and meaning to our lives, and without it, there is suffering."[12] "Driven by shame," Brown continues, "is the fear of not being worthy of real connection." No one would deny the importance of connecting with others, as this devoted researcher has indicated, but at a core level—a deeper existential level—is our need to connect not simply with other people, but with someone more powerful, more essential, more trustworthy, more absolute, and absolutely good: God. Created *by* God and *for* God, our greatest longing is for God. We long to be loved by Him, accepted by Him, and valued by Him. As the Bible indicates:

> "For in Him we live and move and exist ..." (Acts 17:28).
> "For from Him and through Him and to Him are all things" (Romans 11:36).
> "For by Him all things were created ... through Him and for Him" (Colossians 1:16).

And as is written in Psalms, "O, God, You are my God; I shall seek You earnestly; my soul thirsts for you, my flesh yearns for You ..." (Psalm 63:1).

"My soul longed and even yearned for the courts of the Lord; my heart and my flesh sing for joy to the living God" (Psalm 84:2).

Maybe somewhere, the many faces of shame may be traceable to our ultimate need to be accepted and loved by God. Not maybe. Definitely.

Confidence that we belong to God, that we are worthy of His love, is foundational to our very existence. When a person peels away all the human relational disappointment and rejection and looks inward and upward—and does not feel worthy of love, acceptance, and belonging from our Creator God—the long-term effects are overwhelming. Nothing could be worse or more devastating than to question or doubt our acceptability or worth from God.

Why do we doubt? Why do we question? Why does this doubt even exist? What opened the door to the idea that we lack intrinsic worth, that there is a decision to be made or a condition of acceptability or love-worthiness? Where did conditionality of love even begin? Misunderstanding is to blame. And misunderstanding causes shame.

Shame is kryptonite to the human soul.

This soul kryptonite is said to be the root of many dysfunctions in individual lives and families. It is even wreaking havoc within the family of God. We are born with the stamp of our Creator and are created to have an intimate relationship with Him. He knows us best and wants every one of us to know Him and His love. But there is a problem at this most essential core level. We pick up mixed messages and lies along the way. And we transfer these fictitious thoughts—that seem to stick to us like glue—onto God. Somewhere along the way, we have picked up errant beliefs about God. When they are corrected, our new understanding has the potential to resolve shame once and for all.

We all—at least most people I know—come from dysfunctional families. We are imperfect. Try as we might, we make mistakes and send mixed messages (because we learned them somewhere in our past). But our relationship with God should not be wrought with dysfunction and certainly not any semblance of shame. Our soul and spiritual relationship with our Creator is the most significant primal need to address and nurture. Shame is not how our Creator God designed us or made us *tick*. When we experience shame and then connect that shame onto our relationship with God—projecting it onto Him as though it were of His making—we have hog-tied God to a false idea of our intrinsic worthlessness. If we project the lie upon God that His love is conditional, or that it comes to us only when we are love-worthy, we are creating God in our image. The same could be said if we think our love-worthiness is somehow tied to our performance of religious good works. These are just a few reasons errant beliefs like these make life futile.

Author and psychologist Larry Crabb writes that:

> Everyone who takes the blinders off and sees life as it really is in human experience, will be required to choose one of only three options: commit suicide, go mad, or trust God. Those who choose option three must trust God radically and repeatedly, in even the worst of times.[13]

But life has a way of building up walls of inhibition to trust God, let alone others.

Our inhibition to trust God is rooted in our doubt that He considers us worthy of love and that He is loving and good, all the time. It is very hard to trust anyone when you think poorly or incorrectly about them.

But we are either ignorant or project onto God what we learn from our interactions with others. If a boy has a lousy, uncaring father, that boy may very well think his heavenly Father is just like his old man. The boy may project those negative, doubt-filled thoughts and feelings onto God. This is a serious and significant problem—a spiritual problem that requires a spiritual solution. When I say *spiritual*, I mean it is much more than purely psychological or emotional. It is more than a humanistic issue. This is a divine issue. All truth leads back to God; therefore, untruths or lies are rooted somewhere else. When we twist truths and suppose they are from God or are true—in their twisted form—we create an object that is impossible to trust.

Until shame is dealt with at this level—at the level of God—all we will do is dance around the real heart of the problem and deal only with the scars and the sores.

Spiritual shame is a malady we must address at its very core. Shame requires much more than a Band-Aid.

Root Cause

We see the devastating effects of shame and feel its brutal impact, but most of us miss the fact that the cause hides underneath the shame. Shame in itself is not the disease, though it masquerades as one. In order to rid our lives of this infection, we have to attack shame at its root, identifying what it is and where it comes from. Said another way, shame is not the fire, it is the smoke. But to deal with the smoke, we must douse the flames.

If you are sitting around a campfire and you realize your eyes have become itchy and watery, you will, hopefully, realize the smoke is irritating your eyes. You may put drops in your eyes, move away from the fire, adjust your chair, or use your hand as a fan to wave the smoke away. Is the smoke the issue? No, not really. The smoke is the cause of your irritated eyes, but the root cause is the fire. To deal with the smoke, one must put out the fire.

Shame is as destructive as the smoke caused by the fire. But the flames are to blame. The fire is the real problem.

When we talk about shame, we must explore the issue of cause and effect. And then, most importantly, the difference between a cause and *the* cause (root cause).

The effects of shame can be numerous: hiding, depression, lack of self-confidence, self-mutilation, or drug and alcohol addiction. Further effects are performance/people-pleasing and arrogance/superiority. These can all lead to being judgmental and exclusivistic, or ostracizing, shunning, or spurning people or groups. Identifying the out-workings of shame can be helpful to bring attention to and identify the problem and propel one to dig deeper and discover the cause. Effects can be addressed, but addressing the effects is like dressing a wound. Putting a Band-Aid over a sore doesn't deal with the *real* problem, even though it might make life more tolerable or even temporarily enjoyable. Bandages are salves. If healing is required, what needs to be addressed is the wound.

The causes of shame in a person's life can be numerous: poor self-image, upbringing, personal tragedy, and dysfunctional parenting. Sociology and psychology have contributed enormous amounts of facts, data, and insightful research that are helpful in identifying these types of causes. They offer some practical steps to consider the causes, or compensate for and counteract the devastating and debilitating effects of shame.

In my opinion, there is a significant difference between a cause (causal factor) and the root cause. A cause can directly affect the outcome of shame, but that is not necessarily the root cause. Living in shame and feeling like you are unworthy of love because you were raised by a controlling and demeaning father who did not know how to love, may cause shame. But the shortcomings and weaknesses of one's parent is not the root cause; it is merely a causal factor. The root cause is an issue that is much deeper and goes much further back.

In order to eliminate shame, what must be dealt with is the root cause in the causal chain. The root cause (initial cause in causal chain) of shame is an essential matter. Why does shame exist in the world to begin with? Why does the controlling and demeaning father who does not know how to show love act in such a way? What is the fire and how did it ignite?

Heart of the Matter: A Theological Problem

It is so important and critical to address the root cause of shame and find a reliable and permanent solution. Identifying causes, like a dysfunctional parent, and offering alternative perspectives and solutions to counteract the shame can help. But because it fails to deal with the much more important issue of intrinsic worth, it is like waving at the smoke while the fire rages. Shame is an issue of essential worth, so to deal at that level one must get beyond the temporal to the eternal … the divine.

Our intrinsic or essential worth cannot be developed, healed, or sustained if sourced in exterior or finite sources, for such sources are not permanent; they are ever changing. Such is the case if we seek to find intrinsic worth in other people, opinions, creeds, politics, race, or government. Intrinsic worth must come from God, who transcends all and is the source of absolute truth. God does not change, so His view of us and our worth is reliable and eternal. This is essential worth, not conveyed or secondary worth (which is subject to whims). If our perspective of God is wrong, then our belief about our intrinsic worth will be in jeopardy, and our experience of a loving God will be met with serious limitations, hindrances, and hiccups.

If the core of our being longs for a connection with our Creator, then we must be assured that the Creator wants a connection with every human soul. Don't you agree?

Ask yourself:

- Does God create every single human being for relationship with Himself?
- Does God see every human soul as worthy of love and connection?
- Are there conditions that must be met to be considered love-worthy?
- Does conditionality or decision even exist in the love discussion about God?
- Does God see every human having equal opportunity and access to Him?

How we answer these questions and how we view God in this regard, matters immensely. Our standing in this relationship matters more than any other relationship, although it may affect every other relationship either positively or negatively. We must get to the heart of this matter. We must get to the root cause of shame.

I suggest to you that the root cause of shame is our errant view of God (and how we think He views us). Consequently, the solution—dousing the flames—comes from thinking rightly about Him. Solutions are not for symptoms; they are for the source. The source of our shame is our poor perspective of God.

Let me repeat that, for it is critically important. *The source of shame is a poor perspective of God.* Remember, "Shame is the intensely painful feeling or experience of believing that we are flawed and, therefore, unworthy of love and belonging."[14] If we don't know we belong in God's presence and that He created us for Himself, we are all on a slippery slope to shame and shame-based relationships. If we think our intrinsic worth is questionable, that our acceptability to God or our worthiness of being loved by God is even optional (a choice or decision

He must make about us), our trust in God is at risk. Or, if we think His love only extends so far (i.e., has limits), or our performance plays some part, then our faith in God is headed down a very fickle path, and we will live in unholy fear and hiding: *shame*.

Any thought or belief that erodes the confidence that we belong to God and that God sees us as worthy of love and acceptance is wrong and destructive. Anything that destroys our sense of worth and value to God is an error. If God is a picky, hard-to-please, finicky, selective chooser of some for good and others for evil—if even the chance exists that some are chosen and others are not—we have a severe crack in the foundation.

If I think, even for a brief moment, that I am unworthy of love from God or unworthy of belonging to God, it is going to have serious personal ramifications and affect every relationship I experience. And it is going to bring me to deep despair. That kind of despair makes me want to disappear. That is shame.

It is the belief that I am defective in some foundational way. That I am unworthy of love and belonging, and even unworthy of eating food, taking up space, and breathing air. It is the belief that God only loves if certain conditions are met, or His will must be moved or manipulated to love. It is a belief that my worth is not a foregone conclusion.

Trust God?

It is very hard to trust someone if we're not sure how they will respond to us. We ramble around wondering if God is going to choose us for His team or not. We wonder if His love and grace are as extensive and all-encompassing as we know they need to be. We wonder if the good we do is enough. Is it ever enough for worth and acceptance?

To deal with intrinsic worth, we must encounter a God of truth. Sometimes, as we shall see, that requires dispelling some errors in our beliefs about God. We must encounter God truthfully for a right connection to be realized, and shame extinguished.

If the core of our being longs for a connection with our Creator, we must be assured the Creator views us with intrinsic worth and that He wants a connection with *every* human soul. Our standing in this relationship matters more than any other relationship.

If we don't *believe* we belong with and to the One who created us—and believe *all* are worthy of love, acceptance, and belonging—we will inevitably do damage to ourselves and others. If we don't believe God unconditionally loves us, or if we believe He only decides to love some based on certain conditions (even the condition of His will), we awaken the monster of shame and invite it in to shack up in our souls.

Shame is a monster, and you might be surprised to see who is actually feeding this monster. But there is hope.

And if there is hope for me, then there is hope for you.

But first we have to understand where shame comes from.

---

3 C.G. Jung, quoted from carljungdepthpsychology.wordpress.com.

4 Brennan Manning, *All is Grace*, p.51.

5 Ibid., p.51.

6 Dr. Brené Brown, *Listening to Shame* (2012 TED Conference).

7 Webster's II New College Dictionary.

8 Brené Brown is a research professor at the University of Houston, and has devoted many years to research the topic of shame.

9 Quoted from http://www.worldofquotes.com/quote/117394/index.html.

10 Brené Brown, *Daring Greatly*, p.69.

11 Brené Brown, *Daring Greatly*, p.7.

12 Ibid., p.8.

13 Larry Crabb, *Fully Alive*, p.162.

14 Brené Brown, *Daring Greatly*, p.69.

Chapter 2
The Birth of Shame

*Sin hath the devil for its father, shame for its companion,
and death as its wages.*[15]
~ Thomas J. Watson, Sr.

Keb' Mo' is a three-time Grammy award-winning blues musician. His song "Suitcase"[16] is a poignant mixture of light-hearted humor and tragic sadness. The song depicts an all-too-familiar scenario: parents unwittingly handing *baggage*—or *suitcases*—down to their children. These suitcases are full of unresolved issues of fear, rejection, hurt, abandonment, and mistrust. In the song, as in many lives, the unclaimed baggage, or unpacked suitcases, lead to the breakdown of the family, which tragically means new suitcases are packed and readied for the next generation to pick up and carry into their lives.

These suitcases full of trouble get handed down from one generation to the next, but do we ever stop to think about how it all got started? What about that very first suitcase? It had to begin somewhere.

When we think of shame, do we understand that it had a starting place? Do we recognize that it *began* somewhere, at some point in time? Where did it come from? How did we get it? When did the first suitcases of trouble appear?

The problem of shame is an ancestral one. The first two suitcases date back to the beginning and are inscribed with two famous names. But they did not dig out the baggage from the basement; they patented it. And we have been carrying it around ever since.

Where and why did it all begin?

It all started with a lie.

The Birth of Shame: Naked, Baby!
The Bible says that in the beginning "God saw all that He had made, and behold, it was very good" (Genesis 1:31).

Six days of creative work, culminating in the creation of man and woman, and it was *very good*. In the realm of this superlative goodness, it says, "And the man and his wife were both naked and were not ashamed" (Genesis 2:25).

Don't read over that too quickly or dismissively. Those are powerful, ancient words. Naked and *not ashamed*.

Let that sit and resonate for a moment. No clothes and—most importantly—no shame. No suitcase of trouble—*yet*.

Naked shamelessness is a very different picture than what we are used to in our present-day experience. One of the first things we do every single day is to get dressed. We don't even begin to imagine tackling our day before we suit-up in our latest fashions. We wear clothes; it's what we do. And we don't undress until we crawl into bed late in the evening to close the day.

As I write this, I am fully clothed and suspect, as you read, you are as well. At least I hope. The idea of nakedness, especially shameless nakedness, does not easily resonate with us. Even within the privacy of our own homes, our own bedrooms, we do not experience naked shamelessness. It is safe to say that "going commando" is unfamiliar and uncharted territory for most people. There is a connection with this reality and the opening chapters of Genesis.

Adam and Eve were naked and not ashamed, and it was *very good*. This was good in a *good* way, not like a nudist thinks when he finds a nudist colony. This was pure goodness. Nothing demented, nothing evil, nothing selfish, nothing shameful.

It is the visceral part of this equation, "not ashamed," which deserves our fullest attention and consideration. They were without shame. It was not just one good day; this was indicative of their whole existence. No shame. Shame did not exist as we know it. They had no fear of rejection, for that reality did not exist. They did not, or could not, even begin to imagine the intense feelings of not being loved, feeling insecure, or not belonging.

There are very few places in the Bible where the concept of *no shame* appears. This is a unique, but sublime and divine setting. On the other hand, shame, on its own without the *no*, is a whole other story. Shame is everywhere in the Bible and in man's history. It has a way of following us all. It is haunting. But that is not the way life was originally intended when it was *very good*. Nietzsche said that the most humane thing to do for someone is to spare them shame.[17] Shame is *in*humane. It makes perfect sense that our human existence began without it.

At the very moment when Adam and Eve were naked and not ashamed—and it was very good—that was the moment when they were the most human.

Shamelessness is the most sublime of human existence and experience.

Adam and Eve were loved. They belonged and they knew it. There was no doubt God loved them. They were of value to God and His plan, and this value was intrinsic to their *being*, not their *doing*. They did not question God's integrity or goodness. They owned no baggage.

This picture of Adam and Eve in this shamelessness is captivating. It grabs our attention. It shouts to us, yet it seems foreign, like a dialect we don't quite understand. Is there an *app* that can help translate? There must be; there is an *app* for everything. Yet try as we might, it is not that easy. For some reason, which we hope to discover, shame does not vanish easily or go away quietly. And it clouds our judgment.

We all deeply desire and hunger for a life without shame, but it continually evades us. Even if we are serious about searching it out and finding it, it seems elusive and just beyond our grasp. Shamelessness is a kind of Holy Grail ... or Bigfoot. We hear rumors of it. People tell stories of shamelessness sightings, but most have never seen it in person. Sure, there have been stories told and pictures offered as evidence of its existence, but those pictures are blurry and were probably photo-shopped.

Why is shamelessness such an elusive creature?

Everything in me screams out that this is wrong. Shamelessness shouldn't be a proverbial Sasquatch. And I believe I am right to think this way. Shame was not part of our original design.

And it is not part of God's purpose or character.

Everything about who God is and what He does is for our benefit and His glory, so that we might have life and walk in shamelessness. That is why creation began in this *very good* way.

Shamelessness is:

- Acceptance and wholeness
- Security
- Powerful and purposeful
- Liberating
- Motivating
- Fearless
- What we were created to experience
- What God desires for us

Shamelessness is, out of the very mouth of God, "very good" (Genesis 1:31).

Adam and Eve had it. They knew nothing else.

Why were Adam and Eve shameless? Because they were in harmony with God and each other. Man and woman were a team. They had a shared purpose. And they had divine marching orders. They were loved and connected. They had significance. They had the approving thumbs-up from God and to each other. Ideas, thoughts, and beliefs outside of this paradigm did not exist. Oh yes, and they were without sin.

Sin and Sasquatch

There it is, that nasty three letter word: *SIN*. That is where it all went wrong. That is where shamelessness became an elusive Sasquatch. Sin was the culprit. But sin does not just happen. The apostle James wrote, "But each one is tempted when he is carried away and enticed by his own lust {*desire*}. Then when lust has conceived, it gives birth to sin ..." (James 1:14-15). Sin was born into human existence that very day, but something happened before delivery. It started with temptation.

The question is this: Where did the temptation come from? It came from a lie, not a tree with forbidden fruit. The lie came from the snake.

The lie was like the lure that the snake used to entice and carry Adam and Eve away.

The lie was subtly targeted at Adam and Eve's perspective of God. This is the spark that ignites the fire that leads to all the smoke. This is an important distinction to make in the story. Satan enticed Adam and Eve not merely by the fruit, but to think wrongly about God. Satan spun a web of deception that God was not good and that He was keeping important privileges from them because He did not consider them worthy. The thumbs-up had become a thumbs-down. But it was all lies.

God was better at deciding for Adam and Eve what was good and evil. He wasn't keeping something from them because they were unworthy; He was keeping it from them because He loved them and knew they would not be as good at knowing good and evil as He was *for* them. Satan cast out the lure, and they bought the lie—hook, line, and sinker.

The lie was an untruth about the nature of God and His perspective of man. An untruth can be reasonable and believable, but it is still a lie. And man believed the lie, trusting the serpent instead of God.

This is the reason shamelessness vanished. This is the time when the evil counterpart—an evil twin of sorts—of shamelessness entered the human landscape. Their suitcases had arrived, fully packed, with their names monogrammed on the front.

Here is how it went from very good to bad. After eating the fruit, Adam said to God, "I heard the sound of You in the garden, and I was afraid because I was naked; so I hid myself" (Genesis 3:10).

There it is:

- Fear
- Nakedness
- Hiding

Those three create a perfect picture of shame—the true axis of evil. This is exactly what Satan was fishing for that day. Now, none of these three are elusive at all. In fact, we long for them to disappear. But they don't. They hunt us down relentlessly. Sin came as the result of a lie, and shame came as a companion to sin.

This is where errant beliefs about God will lead us.

And the lie and the errant beliefs only got worse, compounded by sin.

What sin and shame did to Adam was cause him to think wrongly about himself and about God. For the first time, Adam thought he was damaged goods and that God was angry and wanted nothing to do with him. Hiding seemed like the only option. Sin and shame create a false reality that intrinsic worth has been lost (or never existed), and that there is now a decision to be made by God as to whether He will consider us worthy of love. Since we don't know the outcome of the choice, and we don't feel worthy of being chosen, we are afraid and hide. This is an attack on the character and nature of God.

Adam felt like he was unworthy and unlovable. He thought he was bad or at least not good enough. And he began to think God would change His mind, or already had, about loving him. So he became unsure as to how God would act from that point forward. Adam felt like God's love was conditional. Unfortunately, through Adam, this condition spreads to all mankind for all time when we follow in the footsteps of sin (Romans 5:12). Shame became a worldwide epidemic. The baggage passed down. Hell in a handbag.

Back to the Garden

There was Adam, and a piece of each one of us, fearful and hiding from God: *ashamed*. At the moment Adam felt he had screwed up too badly to be accepted, he believed he didn't deserve to take up space on the ground he was standing upon. Adam felt he had become damaged goods. Life was over as he knew it. He felt unlovable and like he couldn't face God— or that God may or may not want to face him. Adam wanted to crawl into a hole and die.

Shame grew feet that day. It was humanized.

But it was all based on a false reality.

God had not changed; only Adam's perspective had changed. And his perspective of himself changed as well. This observation is absolutely crucial to the story of shame.

Satan wielded the sword of shame, and it cut a deep wound into Adam and all humanity. Satan was already disconnected from God, so his goal was to ruin our lives by making us feel unworthy of a connection to God by causing us to believe God doesn't love us. Satan sowed disbelief: God could not, or would not, love us unconditionally. This was Satan's experience, and he was now making it ours as well. Misery loves company.

A *very good* beginning was overshadowed by a cloud that rolled in like a thick blanket of fog over all humanity. The feeling of freedom and joy had been smashed upon the rocks of bitter disappointment and despair. Once it was naked and not ashamed; now it is naked, fearful, and fraught with shame.

The tranquil became toxic.

Here is the birth of shame.

It was all based on a lie. Errant beliefs about God are the real problem. Errant beliefs about God lead to a lack of trust in the errant God of our beliefs. The lack of trust in God leads to living life in the sphere of our trespasses and sin, walking through life according to the course of this world and the prince of the power of the air (Ephesians 2:1-2). That is death, the wage of sin (Romans 6:23). Errant beliefs lead us to insecurity, not knowing where we stand with God. Errant beliefs about God's love and grace spread like wildfire. That is not a pretty picture.

If Great, Great Grandpa lived in a home where shame ruled, it is likely that Great Grandpa, Grandpa, and Dad grew up the same way, and that is how I ended up with it as well. Ugly. And this ugliness gets passed down and taught from one generation to the next. We become products of our environment. Sociology and psychology studies confirm this reality. It all began with a lie. It traces back to the Garden in Genesis.

The original lie was this: God is not good, and you will be like God. The result, because it was a trick, was shame. Now I don't really know if I have any intrinsic value, or whether God is good all the time to all people.

Satan's attack was on the character and nature of God, and it led to man becoming jumbled and confused about the God with whom he was created to commune and walk with. Man started to think improperly about God.

When Adam and Eve were in the Garden, they believed a lie about God. The consequence of their action—eating the fruit God told them not to eat—was that they "surely died." This death was the experience of evil, something they had no prior knowledge of. Now, two options exist: life or death, evil or good, light or darkness. In the aftermath of their sin, the Bible says Adam and Eve were thinking improperly about God. What were their thoughts?

- They thought they were now damaged goods; God could not be close to them or love them in their fallen state. The errant belief was that intrinsic value and worth were lost.
- They thought God's love was conditional; God would love them only if they performed well, if they lived as He told them to live.
- They thought God's grace was insufficient to cover them.
- They thought performance was indispensable for a sense of worth, and the lack of performance proves worthlessness.

A.W. Tozer wrote, "There is scarcely an error in doctrine or a failure in applying Christian ethics that cannot be traced finally to imperfect and ignoble thoughts about God."[18]

Our perspective, like Adam before us, is the root cause of shame. All of our baggage can be traced to the Garden. Lost luggage has been located. We think wrongly about God.

Someone once said everyone has baggage, so the key to wholehearted living is finding someone who loves you enough to help you unpack. This is how much God loves us; He helps us unpack. This is why, despite the surplus of luggage of all sorts, shapes, and sizes, shamelessness is available today.

If we cannot get rid of this baggage, how can we expect to help others find healing from shame and be reconciled to the heart of God? The buck stops here. We have to do something about this right now. The church is a place to belong and a house of hope and healing, but if we keep doing what we're doing, we'll get more of what we already have.

Shame is, Brené Brown writes, the "intensely painful feeling or experience of believing that we are flawed and therefore unworthy of love and belonging."

- Shame came from sin.
- Sin did not come from God.
- Shame is not an expression of God.
- And God was not done … thankfully.

We will see that the story did not stop there—man in the bushes separate and hiding—and God did not stop there either. Unfortunately, many of us have wandered from the path, lost our way, and stopped.

---

15 Thomas J. Watson Sr., quoted from thinkexist.com.

16 Keb Mo, *Suitcase*, Epic, 2006.

17 Friedrich Nietzsche, quoted from http://www.brainyquote.com/quotes/quotes/f/friedrichn396470.html.

18 A.W. Tozer, *Knowledge of The Holy*, p.2.

Chapter 3
Rerouting

*Maybe the greatest argument against God
is His people, the church.*[19]
~ A.J. Swoboda

Nowadays, it is nearly impossible to get lost. I said *nearly*.

With the invention of user-friendly GPS devices, smartphones with Google Maps, and navigational apps, pretty much everyone—even the directionally-challenged person—is able to find the way to a desired destination.

As we saw in the last chapter, once Adam believed the lie and ate the fruit from the tree of the knowledge of good and evil, he was immediately shackled with shame. Adam hid because he was afraid and ashamed. He was afraid because he no longer believed God could be trusted to be good. He was ashamed because he thought God would look at him as if he were damaged goods and intrinsically worthless. Adam now thought God was conditional in His love and acceptance. Adam was lost.

And we are no better off than Adam. In fact, we may be even worse off.

With all that is available to ground ourselves in Truth, it is surprisingly easy for us, nonetheless, to get lost and find ourselves hiding in the bushes. It is just as easy, if not more so, for us to become darkened in our thoughts about God.

Biblically speaking, we have lost the way.

To deal with shame, we must get back on the road to thinking rightly about God. Shame came from sin, and sin came from lies about God. In order to reverse this, we must regain proper thinking. Like Tozer said, "There is scarcely an error in doctrine or a failure in applying Christian ethics that cannot be traced finally to imperfect and ignoble thoughts about God."[20]

Our ethics are failing. Our theology is failing.

All because we are thinking wrongly about God.

Alister E. McGrath made an accurate assessment of how this happens when he wrote, "Theology has lost its moorings in the Bible, and prefers to conduct its disputes with reference to systematic theologians of the past, rather than by direct engagement with biblical texts."[21] It is so easy to lose our way and end up somewhere we never intended to be if we are not anchored to the Scriptures. Errant beliefs lead us astray into shame.

Shame originated from a lie: deception. And the lie won't die because *we* feed it. Who's the *we*? God's people, the church, you and me; we are the *we*. We feed the lie, and we may not even realize we are doing it.

Irony of Ironies

What the church has done, even if unknowingly, is foster the same untruths that were troubling Adam, and we have done so under the guise of truth: doctrine. Sure it sounds better and more dignified because we have fancy names for this "truth," but when you boil it all down, it is the same old untruth. And the result is the same: paralyzing, disorienting shame.

The initial lie was compounded into all sorts of untruths and false beliefs about God. In an irony of all ironies, these lies that found their way into the Garden (human experience) have found their way into the church. These errant beliefs have become the basis of traditional, Christian orthodoxy. Yes, you read that correctly. When you boil down the traditional teachings of the church, one discovers that lying beneath, buried deep down, are the same old destructive and harmful lies.

You may not be aware of this or know the fancy names to these doctrines, but the odds are you have been affected by them in one way or another. And maybe you are infecting others without even knowing you are causing harm and spreading shame.

The majority of Protestants (Lutherans, Presbyterians, Baptists) and Catholics believe and teach others some version of the following doctrines:

- Man is born totally depraved, dead, and incapable of doing good or responding to God. He is deserving of hell: eternal torment of God's wrath. Man is born that way.
- Any man is saved only because God chose him before the foundation of the world. God predetermines and chooses who will be saved and who will rot in hell. Many believe God chooses some and merely passes over others, leaving them to get what they deserve.
- God only savingly loves the ones whom He has chosen. Christ died only for these chosen ones. There is a limit to the efficacy (not the sufficiency) of Christ's death.
- Only those who perform well prove their worth, and God will only accept into heaven those who persevere in a life of good works.

These beliefs (or doctrines) about God, once you boil them down, have exactly the same effect on us as they did on Adam and Eve when Satan deceived them in the Garden through his lies. What these doctrines do is make us doubt God's character and our own worth.

When we doubt the goodness of God and His valuation of us, we invite the monster of shame in the front door. But we do more than doubt. We believe these lies. This is the root cause of shame.

It is not necessary to poke any one specific person, scholar, denomination, or seminary in the theological eye, for that would be divisive, polemic, and unnecessary. Truth will prevail.

If, as the theology experts say, man is born damaged, dead, and damned, then he can only become worthy if God chooses him. That means no intrinsic worth exists. According to many of these experts, what man deserves—because he lacks all intrinsic worth—is an eternity separate from God in a place called hell. Even if God does choose some and not others, the ones not chosen are essentially worthless. What does this say about man's intrinsic worth? Or, worse yet, what does it say about God?

If there is a decision to be made as to who will be loved, then all are not intrinsically lovable. If it comes down to a decision (a choice) by God—no matter when that decision took place or the basis upon which that decision was made—we have destroyed our perception of intrinsic worth because we don't know whom God will choose. We can't even be sure we have been chosen or are capable of being chosen. We may try to perform, or we may assume He has chosen us and not others. We might simply suffer the ping-pong effect between doubt and conviction.

Divine choosing of individuals is inherently shameful. If choice exists, then non-choice also exists. If this is true in the lovability of human beings, we have a serious issue. If our intrinsic worth is conditioned upon our performance, our confidence in God's character will be as whimsical as our moods.

Consider for a moment the issue of being chosen. Shame can be the flip side of the coin *chosen* or *worthy*. Think back to days of youth when you were standing in the gym or on the ball field and the typical scenario begins to play itself out. The best two athletes are automatically the captains who choose their teams. If you are one of those two, you are already chosen, and you have no more worries, except to make sure you get the best players on your team. But if you aren't one of those two, you are any one of the other students waiting, hoping, and praying your name will quickly be called. Inevitably, because that's how this thing goes, there is always someone who is last. And that last person is never actually chosen at all. He just has to go to the team that is to pick next by default. That stings. Or, worse yet, if you are the "odd man out," it means you are very clearly NOT CHOSEN to either team. The odd man out is certainly not good enough. That really stings.

This idea applied to God has enormous potential for undue pain and suffering. This erroneous teaching that the church has promoted for hundreds of years has left—and continues to leave—a trail of dead bodies in its wake.

This destruction of intrinsic or essential worth spreads death: the experience of evil, fear, and hiding from God. It is the unceasing cycle of shame that originated in the Garden as a result of Satan's deception. This is why so many people remain in hiding and are afraid.

We might have lost our way. We might be completely messed up in how we are thinking about God. But the journey is not over. As long as we have breath, there is hope.

Free Indeed

The Bible lays claim to a power of its own to sanctify (John 17:17) and to free (John 8:32) because it is the Son, the Word, who sets us free (John 8:36a). And whom the Son sets free is free indeed (John 8:36b).

Freedom is what we need most desperately. It comes from thinking rightly about God. We have lost our way, but there is a road home. That road is called Truth.

Vincit Omnia Veritas! Yes, it's Latin. Don't panic. I had to look it up too. It means *Truth Conquers All Things!*

The only way to combat lies and the bondage those lies cause is with Truth.

But this begs the question: *truth about what?*

Does the truth of astronomy help set me free of shame? Does truth about biology, mathematics, or philosophy help liberate me from my feeling of worthlessness?

No, because shame is not biological, mathematical, or philosophical. And while shame is an "astronomical" problem, the problem is not astronomical, if you get what I mean.

What we need is a word of truth from the source of all Truth.

Freud and Jung theorized the father complex, a strong impulse or association related to the image or archetype of a father.[22] This was Freud's and Jung's way of giving people an explanation or understanding of why they do the things they do. I would suggest that to go beyond explaining behavior, the pathway of liberation and significance is a much more divine dilemma, directly related to how we think about God the Father, and how we think He thinks about us. That is a theological issue. That is a heavenly Father issue. Thus, the only way to combat the lie and shame is to discover truth from *the* source.

God is our source, but if we continue to hold errant beliefs about Him that go untested and unchecked, our father-complex is doomed to the fate that has been created for us. But we can wonder. We can question. We can rethink and reshape our perspective of God according to the Truth He has given. To do this, we must consider how we think about God, and how we believe God thinks about / views us, which is really just another way we think about God and His nature or character.

Author and certified interventionist Jeff VanVonderen gets to the heart of this issue:

> God is our source. He is our need-meeter, our vindicator, our defender, the one who has the last word on our value and acceptance. Other people can think whatever they want—and they will. What they say might feel hurtful sometimes, but they do not decide the truth about us, God does.[23]

God decides the truth about us. And it goes without saying that God decides the truth about Himself. In the Bible, He lets us share in these truths. Psychology and sociology can help identify the problem and offer guidance as to how to live differently. Theology—our thoughts about God—is absolute, and God has the last word.

Right thinking about God and His evaluation of us will address our shame. And here are the reasons. We can't go back and change our parents, and we can't go back and explain them away and still be set free. We could go back and analyze every generation of every family who has ever lived. But after all the research and analysis is complete, we are still left with these questions: What will we believe is true about us? Who are we? Are we valuable? And are we worthy of love and belonging? Even after all the help we can gain from psychology or sociology, those questions remain to be answered. We may still doubt or question our worth because we lack a positive source of authoritative truth about our worthiness.

We can't change our past or the environment in which we were raised. All of these factors may have been quite imperfect. What we *can* do is understand that the most important perspective about us and our worth is ultimately and appropriately God's. We can understand that our worth should never come from imperfect people raised by imperfect people, but from a perfect God who created us and loves us as our heavenly Father.

- God is our Creator.
- God is our Father.

- God is the source of Truth.

The damage from holding erroneous beliefs is hurtful. Believing lies is damaging to our physical beings. Board certified Christian psychiatrist Timothy R. Jennings, M.D., writes:

> When we believe lies about God, those false beliefs actually damage us, change our neural circuits, and warp our minds and characters.[24]

Lies leave a mark. You can see how this can wreak havoc on our Father-God complex. The longer we believe erroneous thoughts about God, the more we are allowing a negative groove to wear deeper and deeper into our minds.

Is there any question why God would be against some of the prophets of old who would "use their tongues and declare, 'The Lord declares,'" when He had not at all declared what these prophets wanted to preach (Jeremiah 23:31)? As God was against such prophets in the history of Israel, He must be against them throughout the history of the church when they declare false words leading "my people astray by their falsehoods and reckless boasting … they do not furnish this people the slightest benefit" (Jeremiah 23:32). Unfortunately, this same thing continues to happen in our day.

We need true words on this subject from God.

There is no greater need than to know we are worthy, acceptable to God, loved, and lovable. God unconditionally loves *all*, and there is enough of Him and His love to go around for *all*. This is the path to shame-free living. This is the firm foundation from which true wholehearted living is derived.

Before we proceed, first a request … a summons of sorts.

An Invitation

How do we continue down a path of growth and increase in knowledge?

The greatest and most essential element necessary for the growth of knowledge is to come to the table of learning with the assumption that what we believe in the present (or have believed in the past) could be wrong. It is acceptable to question, to wonder, and even to doubt.

You read that correctly. It is acceptable. In fact, it is necessary to question, wonder, and doubt.

I read a quote recently that said, "Not all who wander are lost."[25]

I understand what this author was getting at with this statement. In our present day, we equate strong faith—or a mature Christian—with psychological certainty about Truth. This is what the church calls orthodox doctrine. To question these core beliefs is not something that is fostered or encouraged, but is greatly needed. To wonder about these truths does not mean we are lost. It is safe to explore.

Come to the table.

Lies that don't die tend to multiply. The lie continues to fester and frustrate to this day. We can give the lies fancy-sounding names and associate them with esteemed historical figures of the past, or give creditability to them because of past "official" judgments of men. But in the end, a lie is still a lie.

Yet lies will die if they are not fed. But feed them we do. And the devastation continues because lies are destructive.

Are you open to looking at something you may think is truth but may be a lie nevertheless? Will you consider the facts with openness, even openness to being wrong? I can personally attest that the journey is worthwhile to let go and welcome what comes.

Will you come to the table?

What Will We Find?

We will consider the Bible does *not* say that man is born utterly damaged, dead, or deserving of eternal damnation. The Bible says:

- Man has the capability to trust God and will be held accountable for not doing so.
- God has chosen some for the purpose of particular service. He has chosen all for some service. But He does not choose some to go to heaven while a mass majority of others are chosen to rot in hell.
- God loves the whole world, and Christ died for the whole world.
- God's love knows no bounds. God's love is limitless.

The Bible says following after God is important, but not for the reasons the church has wrongly emphasized.

- There is far too much hiding.
- There is far too much people-pleasing and performance-based living.
- There is far too much religious schizophrenia.
- There is far too much arrogance, judgmentalism, and condemning.
- There is far, far too much shame.

We are like ships adrift at sea, but most of the captains and passengers have no idea they are lost and heading for an iceberg. We don't need to consult more books of theology; we need to engage prayerfully with our God and His Word.

The first step in finding our way is admitting we could be lost.

Yes, we *must* be lost. If we are filled with shame and that shame has caused the breakdown of vital relationships, we have all the signs of being adrift.

The traditional route we are on is not a good one. It will not get us to His desired destination for us. It is not efficient or effective. We have lost our way and must adjust, like the adjustment made by mapping/navigational software on our phones when we are lost or have taken a wrong turn: *Rerouting*.

You might be shocked how easily the wrong beliefs go away when you see the Truth.

19 A.J. Swoboda, *Messy*, p.160.

20 A.W. Tozer, *Knowledge of The Holy*, p.2.

21 Alister E. McGrath, *Iustitia Dei*, p.420.

22 http://en.wikipedia.org/wiki/Father_complex.

23 Jeff VanVonderen, *Families Where Grace is in Place*, p.143.

24 Timothy R. Jennings, *The God Shaped Brain*, p.63.

25 A.J. Swoboda, *Glorious Dark*, p. 166.

Chapter 3.9
A Word Before the Word

We are hardwired for connection with God. We are created in His image. We are created for sharing connection, for sharing intimacy. The apostle Paul said, "For in Him we live and move and exist" (Acts 17:28). Paschal talks about a God-shaped vacuum that cannot be filled, try as we might, with anything or anyone but God Himself.

Since it is true we are created to connect with God, we get our sense of worthiness and belonging from God. But if the messages in my head are anything like these, it will be very difficult, if not impossible, to trust God and others:

- You are no good.
- You can do no good; nothing you do will ever be good enough.
- No one will ever love you.
- You don't deserve success or happiness.

No trust, no relationships, and no life because there is no connection to God.

If these messages are wrong—if the beliefs I am built upon are wrong, and I can correct them and replace them with new beliefs—then I am able to engage in life and allow myself to be seen. I will no longer be shackled with shame and fear of rejection. If I know God accepts me, then who can possibly be against me (Romans 8:31)? People may reject me, hurt me, tear me down, but if I know my worth and value are rooted in God—and what He thinks of me and sees in me—then I have an unshakable foundation, one made for living freely.

While I wish correct thinking came naturally or automatically, it does not. We live in a broken world. We grow up in families that have dysfunction (we all have dysfunctional families at some level). Consequently, we can be mean and selfish, lonely and self-pitying. We live in a world full of people who don't know they are loved, and *hurting people hurt people*. This is why we are in need of transforming our minds (Romans 12:1-2; 2 Corinthians 3:18), even if that means adjusting beliefs we have been told are right and true.

What we think matters immensely because it directly affects who we think we are and how we live. As the Proverb goes, "For as he thinks within himself, so is he" (Proverbs 23:7). According to this clear statement, how we think *determines* who we are and how we live. The Christian message, the good news—according to most experts—begins by conveying that every man born into the world is scum: *damaged, dead, and damned.* If that is what you think, then that is what you are. And that will determine how you feel. Naturally, you are going to be afraid. But we are not what *they* say. They, the experts and scholars, have it wrong. God does not think of you in the way they suggest.

If our thinking is based on what God thinks, and if God's thoughts are good and right, then our thinking will be right, and we will be right. Right-thinking people are those who understand God's perspective of man's worth and intrinsic value, and their role in God's plan.

Brené Brown found this out in her years of research:

> Shame works like termites in a house. It's hidden in the dark behind the walls and constantly eating away at our infrastructure, until one day the stairs suddenly crumble. Only then do we realize that it's only a matter of time before the walls come tumbling down.[26]

If we don't deconstruct and tear down the house of cards that is mainstream belief about the nature and destiny of man, those theological termites will slowly eat away at our worth, and the walls will come tumbling down and bury us deeply in shame. But deconstruct we can. And we can rebuild a right perspective developed from the Bible, from God's thoughts.

Here is how we are going to do this.

Bible Forward to Back and Inside Out

In order to correct errant beliefs and develop a biblical or right belief, there are some basic rules and ideas to follow. We do not start outside the Bible. We do not begin in theology or philosophy. Just as importantly, we do not start from the back of the Bible, meaning the New Testament, and then read backward (into the Old Testament) with our theology driving the bus. In order to develop a proper perspective that manifests a proper but developing continuity, we start at the beginning—from the front of the Bible—and read it like any other book, from front to back. We do not start with our theology, because, if we do, then we have brought our bias to the Bible, searching for a place to make it fit. Rather, we start with the Bible and see what theological understandings are born from our reading. We do not start in the New Testament, cherry-picking verses that have been taught to us, pregnant with theological meaning given to them, and then force those ideologies and theologies into other cracks and crevices of the Bible.

If you start with an idea or teaching and bring it back to the Bible, you will find support for that idea or teaching because you were looking for a reason to find it in what you're reading. The danger of this approach is apparent. It's similar to the power of suggestion.

If I tell you I have a slice of apple for you but ask you to close your eyes and then have you hold it, smell it, and eat it, it's likely you will think it was an apple—while all the while it was a pear or even a potato. The power of suggestion, a preconceived belief, confused your mind. You brought into the situation—or rather I did and gave it to you—an idea you then placed over the data your senses were collecting.

If you start with a belief about the meaning of spiritual death, for example—which may have been taught to you early in your spiritual journey and thought by you at the time to be adequately supported by a few New Testament verses—when you turn to the Old Testament and read stories like that of Adam and Eve in the Garden of Eden, you will, almost certainly, read that preconceived idea into their story. You think your interpretation is biblical because you presume your idea of death is correct and must be the meaning of death in this Old Testament story. You force it into the story, rather than allowing the meaning to come from the story naturally and then influence how you understand later verses on spiritual death. If we read the Bible from front to back and from inside out, letting theology be a by-product of our reading, not vice versa, we might end up with very different conclusions.

Over the course of this book, we will be coming back to the Genesis story over and over again because this is the place where the story began. We need to fully know this story and how it shapes our understanding of later passages because those later passages have been used (or misused) to build the house of cards. We have to open our eyes and see if we are eating an apple, a pear, or a potato.

Decision

As we have already said, shame is not the root of the problem, it is the effect. The problem is that we have misunderstood God. Misunderstandings are not misunderstandings to those who hold those beliefs because whatever one believes, he believes it to be right. Right?

To say a variety of opinions exists on theological subjects is to state the obvious. So how do you decide? How do you choose which perspective is right? You step back, read, listen, and pray. You weigh and consider which propositions make the most sense in the passages under consideration, and which make the most sense in light of the whole. You think about the potential pitfalls and advantages of one belief over another. You pick the one that makes the most sense to you (and the Holy Spirit), and then you keep moving forward, always willing to reconsider your conclusion and weigh other ideas and perspectives.

If shame is to have a short shelf life, we must think rightly about God. If we are serious about being set free from shame and the part we play in transferring it, we must be willing to have honest dialogue and engage in open, in-depth, and thorough discussions about what the Bible reveals about God and His evaluation of each of us. It will require some deep thought, prayer, and honest study, the aim being a more biblical and accurate view of God and our own worth. The result of our study will extinguish the flaming fire of shame.

The key to understanding this issue, which unlocks wonderful and profound biblical truth, is so simple that once you see it, you will wonder how anyone ever missed it.

If we don't begin thinking properly about God, we will never think properly about ourselves or others. If we don't allow truth to transform and liberate us, we will continue to eke out whatever meager existence we can muster under this dark shadow of shame.

Are you open to the house of cards to come tumbling down? Are you ready to consider a new perspective?

Onward.

---

26 Brené Brown, *Daring Greatly*, p. 189.

Chapter 4
Damaged

A vase that has held beautiful roses though now broken, will nevertheless hold something of the fragrance it once contained.[27]
~ A.W. Tozer

Sticks and stones may break my bones, but words will never hurt me. Really? What about words from someone you love and respect saying, "You are damaged goods!"

What about from a father?

Remember what Mike heard? *You are worthless!*

Those were not the exact words spoken, but that was the message Mike heard. Like so many who grew up with shaming parents, he lived with the memory of his father telling him he was a waste, and in his case, of genetic fluid. Mike later came to understand and accept that his dad was not on a conscious mission to destroy or hurt him, even though that was the impact.

Sadly, the same can't be said for everyone whose parents feel inconvenienced or burdened by their children and treat them harshly or hurtfully. Other parents deliberately suppress and demean their children, hoping it will toughen them up and make them hard workers. Some dads pick apart every game or performance, point out every mistake or mishap (while avoiding all the positives) in order to "make them better," they say. Some moms detail every physical flaw in their daughter to compel her to match the images in the pages of magazines or Hollywood movies. Even if parents are attempting to make their children better, when they miss the good already present in their child, they are inevitably telling them they aren't good enough. At least that is what is heard. Or, as in Mike's case, *you are no good at all!*

Regardless of the motivation or intention, the effect or impact of driving the message of shame is the same: destruction of worth.

We don't need someone to explain away our abusive fathers or help us reason that it is not our fault, although both cognitive processes might be helpful. What we need is to know the truth about who we really are, because once we understand our worth, the lies will fall away.

Once the voices of self-blame, false accusations, and self-condemnation meet face-to-face with our God-given worth, those voices are silenced.

Ravi Zacharias points out that, "Laws are created to force people to value the life and freedom of other individuals, but the intrinsic dignity of human life can only truly come from God, the Creator, who gives us essential worth."[28] Society needs laws to help protect people's rights because many—like the thief, murderer, or rapist—do not value other human beings or consider them worthy enough to respect and to not violate. Lack of a belief in intrinsic worth often leads to violence. Laws governing society may help protect some and deter others, but they don't heal the human heart. Human beings are not reliable sources of human dignity and worth.

Because this is true, it is plainly evident how difficult it would be to establish intrinsic worth by committee or popular opinion. The "intrinsic dignity of human life can only truly come from God ... who gives essential worth," continues Zacharias. God gives this worth to His creatures because He has the right to do so as our Creator. His assessment of our worth is reliable, trustworthy, and does not change ... for "God is the same yesterday, today, and forever" (Hebrews 13:8). Our worth ascribed by God is essential worth that is different than "conveyed or secondary worth" and is not affected by time or the transitory and fickle nature of man.

So, to the Source we go. And here is what we find.

God Says …

Man is unique. This is not like saying that something is interesting, which could mean either positive or negative. Man is gloriously and wondrously unique in all creation, for God created man "in His image" (Genesis 1:26, 27). When God made man, He chose a mold He had not used before and would not use again on anything else: Himself.

Theologians may debate and quibble about what specifically "the image of God" is, but this does not detract from the point that we are made by Him, to be like Him. We are unlike everything else, and with nothing else do we share that distinction. This is true of every human being who has ever or will ever exist and speaks volumes to incredible and wonderful essential worth.

In addition, man is distinct from other living things because God "breathed into his nostrils the breath of life" (Genesis 2:7). Our engine runs on God's wind; we are wind-turbine engines. We get life from God. God is the creator and sustainer of life (Colossians 1:17, Hebrews 1:3). And if that is not enough, man is unique and exalted in the purpose God gave him to rule and subdue the earth (Genesis 1:26, 28). Mankind has been given the greatest and most important objective of any creature God has made. We are His vice-regents. Man, and all that God created, was "very good" (Genesis 1:31).

We are created by God. We are created in God's image. We have life directly from God. We have a regal and royal purpose that is ours alone.

Very good!

East of Eden

I know what you are thinking. You are saying to yourself, "That is true, but that was before Paradise was lost. All that was before the *Fall*." Well, since you are wondering, are you really sure the Fall *totally* changed the nature of man? Is that what these chapters of Genesis tell us, or is this what our theology about the Genesis story tells us? Did the Fall change man's intrinsic value or worth? If you are like so many others, you suffer from serious doubts about your capability, value, and worth because you have heard for far too long that because of the Fall, you—being born in the likeness of Adam—were born as damaged goods. That is orthodox theology speaking, not God. I'd like to present another option for you to consider.

In the beginning, God told Adam and Eve not to eat the fruit from the tree of the knowledge of good and evil—a simple system of law but absolutely necessary. Yet man failed. What happened that day when Adam and Eve *fell*?

How far did they fall? Were Adam and Eve, in their new fallen state, so damaged they were incapable of responding to God? When God made noises in the Garden and called out to man saying, "Where are you?" and "Have you eaten from the tree?" He did so knowing full well where they were and what they had done. He wanted Adam and Eve to respond to Him. Just as importantly, He gave them the opportunity to respond because they were completely capable of doing so. They had the ability to come out of the bushes, break free of the shame the serpent had shackled them with, and respond to God.

Leave theology aside and read the story yourself. Let the story tell you what is true.

And notice something important when you read it. While they were estranged from God as they hid from Him, God did not turn His back on them, leave them, or give up on them. He was still pursuing them, calling out to them, and talking to them. I believe that if God has any integrity—and, of course, He has *all* integrity—then He would not call out to man, giving him a chance to respond if man were suddenly so damaged he could not respond.

Additionally, the Lord made garments of skin for them, and I am pretty sure it is safe to say it's not because God is bashful. He knew what they needed to feel good: to be covered, protected, and confident enough to continue to worship and walk with Him. After that, God sent them out of the Garden so they wouldn't eat from the tree of life and live forever. Adam and Eve were separated from the Garden of Eden, but not from God. Is it possible to see this separation from the Garden and the Tree of Life as a demonstration of God's wisdom and grace? If it is, then physical death is a *good thing* for it keeps us from living forever in a state in which we are in a spiritual battle to choose good over evil. Either way, they were sent out of the Garden, BUT GOD WENT WITH THEM! Why? Because God was still committed to them, and they were still valuable to God. They were still considered intrinsically worthy, with the capacity for good and the ability to fulfill their original commission, even after the Fall.

After Adam and Eve had been escorted out of the Garden, they began a family of their own. Even if some maintain that Adam and Eve were still good, all hope is shattered in their children, who, according to most theologies, were born in sin and totally damaged persons. Adam and Eve's first two children were named Cain and Abel. On one occasion, God had regard for Abel's offering but not for Cain's offering (Genesis 4:4-5). This made Cain angry, so the Lord said to Cain, "Why are you angry? And why has your countenance fallen?" (Genesis 4:6). Notice here that God is in relationship with Cain, as He was with Abel, Adam and Eve, and presumably with all those living East of Eden. The story indicates the state of Cain's anger and fallen countenance was a momentary experience and not indicative of his whole existence or life.[29] Apparently, Cain had the capacity to respond properly, for God said, "If you do well, will not your countenance be lifted up?" (Genesis 4:7a). Cain also had the capacity to succumb to sin and evil: "And if you do not do well, sin is crouching at the door; and its desire is for you, but you must master it" (Genesis 4:7b). Both options existed for Cain.

Whether the door at which sin is crouching is outside man or inside is irrelevant in the big picture. If man has a nature that is susceptible to sin or is by nature sinful, man still has the capacity to trust God and conquer sin. God told Cain sin wanted dominion over him, but that he should—because he *could*—master (in Hebrew, *mashal*) it. How else could we make sense of this other than to simply accept that God expected Cain to obey Him and conquer sin because God knew he had the capacity to do so? How could God call out to Cain and admonish him to "master sin" if Cain did not have the capacity to respond to God or to actually accomplish what God was calling him to do? It would put God in a bad light if He gave such a command, knowing full well Cain could not obey it because he was not capable. So the opposite must be true: Cain *could* respond to God. Cain *could* have mastered sin. How? By faith. By trusting God. By submitting to God and not to sin—or Satan. All the privileges God had given Adam and Eve in creation, their descendants after them could experience by faith.

Were Cain and Abel born damaged? Were they incapable of doing good? Were they only capable of evil? Cain had more than one option. Cain did not have to choose evil as if that were his only possible choice—as if his corrupt and damaged nature was doomed to sin. After the Fall, the landscape changed significantly (to include a spiritual darkness), and man had an inherited nature, in the likeness of Adam, which is anything but perfect or unchangeable. It was a nature that could crave what God had forbidden, just like Adam and Eve's nature did when they desired the forbidden fruit of that tree. One taste and man was hooked. But like all addictions, it is a choice to imbibe or not, to inhale or not, to touch or not. We've been told for so long that we are born in sin and that our only option is to sin because our nature is predisposed to disappoint God. But is that really how God created us?

Even after the devastation of the flood, God's disciplinary action upon wickedness, the image of God is not marred or nonexistent, for its existence in man is the basis for Noahic law against murder (Genesis 9:6). The reason a life should not be taken, according to this law, is because every single person is an image-bearer of God. This is value, and this value is intrinsic long after the Fall.

Now let's jump ahead a few more years.

Many years after the Fall, David writes a song of praise that gets at the heart of man's worth. David begins the song by asking a question we all ask in one way or another and at some time or another: "What is man that you take thought of him, and the son of man that you care for him?" To David, man is, as a creature of God, something God takes thought of, remembers and cares for (Psalm 8:4). Even though we are created "lower than angels,"[30] God says we are crowned with "glory and majesty" (Psalm 8:5). What is apparent is that man—far east of Eden—is to be praised. Despite man's fallen humanity, he is not so marred or depraved that he is incapable of fulfilling his destiny. And he has certainly not lost his dignity.

Ron Allen observed this reality when he wrote, "This view of the wonders that man may do in praise of God is not presented in ignorance of the wickedness of man—no more so than to suggest David was unaware of man's wickedness when he wrote Psalm 8."[31] Certainly, we do wicked things, and in some cases it characterizes us. But our value and dignity are not lost, nor is our regal purpose set aside.

God speaks to us about our essential worth in the poems of the Book of Psalms, maybe because poetry is a language of love and speaks directly to our hearts. In Psalm 139, David pens these words celebrating God's presence: "For you formed my inward parts; You wove me in my mother's womb. I will give thanks to You, for I am fearfully and wonderfully made; wonderful are Your works, and my soul knows it very well" (Psalm 139:13-14). Fearfully and wonderfully made. David acknowledges in his praise to God that man is separate and distinct from all other created things or beings.[32] That, in and of itself, is a praise. When David phrases his praise around the idea that we are "fearfully made," he is, in Hebrew, saying we are awesome.[33]

To acknowledge this is to praise God.

This obviously applies East of Eden, long after the Fall.

Apples and Oranges

It is common in our day and age to define someone or categorize them by vocation. One of the most common initial questions asked in new introductions is "What do you do?" This seems odd because the most important question should be "Who are you?" We make the same mistake in religious circles as well. We think it is fair and right to categorize and classify people based on what they do or don't do. We talk about believers and unbelievers, Christians and non-Christians, lost or saved, adulterers, alcoholics, and addicts. But we are human *beings,* not human *doings.* What we do is not who we are. The two are different issues altogether.

Apples and oranges.

At least they are to God.

God has a very positive and affirming perspective of His creatures, and He never changes His perspective of our *being* even when our *doing* is inconsistent with Him or His created purpose for us. Even when our behavior becomes so consistent that it is characteristic of our existence, it is not indicative of our essence.

Let me repeat this last statement for it seems too easily lost in Christian thinking. *Even when our behavior becomes so consistent that it is characteristic of our existence, it is not indicative of our essence.*

When we read statements about man's experience, we need to be very careful not to make those statements indicative of his existence or essence. Verses like the following have been misused this way:

- "The heart is more deceitful than all else and is desperately sick; who can understand it?" (Jeremiah 17:9)
- "And all our righteous deeds are like a filthy garment." (Isaiah 64:6)

If I had a nickel for every time I have heard these verses quoted to denigrate the essence of all mankind, I could enter early retirement. The solution to the misuse of these passages and others like them is really quite simple. These passages are describing people (i.e., specifically the nation of Israel) in a particular state of experience in a particular point of time historically.

There is no denying that the people Isaiah describes, for example, had fallen pretty low when he writes, "All our righteous deeds are like a filthy garment." But Isaiah is describing a disobedient people who are going to be disciplined by the Lord before they can experience the glorious future God has planned for them (Isaiah 65-66). Isaiah is not describing the capacity or capability of all of humanity. Jeremiah, when he writes "The heart is more deceitful than all else and is desperately sick," is describing a very similar situation in the history of the nation of Israel on the heels of King Josiah's reforms to cleanse the land of idolatrous worship and bring the nation back to a right walk with Yahweh.

Historical, not universal. Experience, not essence.

These verses describe an experience of man when he lives outside of fellowship with God and His purposes. That does not mean this is the sum total of what man is. What is being described is man's *experience* (his *doing*), not his *being*. Obviously, Israel had done great works previously, so not all their deeds were filthy. Certainly, there are plenty of examples of people in Israel's history, as in the history of humanity, who had good hearts. Otherwise, why would God look on the inside while man looks at the outside (1 Samuel 16:7)? God looks on the inside because the heart is what matters. If there is anything good, it begins in the heart.

Another favorite *club* commonly used to beat down man into *homo sapien* pulp is Genesis 6:5 which reads, "Then the Lord saw that the wickedness of man was great on the earth, and that every intent of the thoughts of his heart was only evil continually."

Once again, this is describing a particular historical situation—not the condition of every heart as it comes forth from the womb. Obviously, according to this verse, man's heart can *become* corrupt. Have you ever wondered why Jesus was so favorable toward children? There is good reason Jesus told His disciples things such as:

- "Unless you are converted and become like children ..." (Matthew 18:3)
- "Whoever then humbles himself as this child ..." (Matthew 18:4)
- "Whoever does not receive the kingdom of God like a child will not enter it at all." (Luke 18:17)

There is something pure and innocent in children that we seem to lose with age—and sin. Obviously, we are not born that way. If every thought of every child was evil continually, why would Jesus tell His learners to be like children and not to hinder them from coming to Him?

Genesis 6:5 describes a certain situation in the history of man. It does not describe the nature and essence of man or the condition of his heart when he is born, or even after he sinned once, twice, three times, or more. Man got to the point in his experience where it could be said of all: "Every intent of the thoughts of his heart was only evil continually." This was true of all the men living at that time, all men except Noah and possibly his family (Genesis 6:8-9, 18).

Noah is actually exhibit A for the defense council that Genesis 6:5 is not meant to describe man's essential nature. Man's heart can become corrupt the longer he walks in death. But even when this becomes a fair and right description or characterization of his heart, he is never without the ability to change his thinking and do what is right in trusting God.

Experience, not essence. This is what happens when man lives apart from God, or God allows man to go his own way (Romans 1:24, 26, 28 and Acts 14:16-17). *Doing* versus *being*. It is absurd to reason that man is worthless and can do no good just because he is not presently doing good at that particular moment or during a prolonged season of his life. The wickedness of man does not rob man of the essential dignity of being a human being created by God, for God, and in the image of God. When man lives contrary to his created worth and purpose, his experience is wanton and wasted, yet he himself is still the wonderful work God has created, designed, and loves. And he is still capable of doing good and trusting God.

If we live in darkness, believe the lies, or walk in the sphere of death, then our doing is wrong, but *we* are not wrong in our essence or being. Even when God told Israel, "the whole head is sick, and the whole heart is faint" (Isaiah 1:5b), God also gave them the remedy for their situation: "Wash yourselves, make yourselves clean; remove the evil of your deeds from My sight. Cease to do evil, learn to do good; seek justice, reprove the ruthless; defend the orphan, plead for the widow" (Isaiah 1:16-17). If they would do as He instructed them to do, He promised: "Though your sins are as scarlet, they will be as white as snow" (Isaiah 1:18).

How Far Did They Fall?

A predominant belief in the church is that the first sin by Adam resulted in something called "original sin," which says all humanity fell sinful that day and became depraved in nature ... worthless, not able to do good, think good, or feel anything good. Louis Berkhoff wrote that it is "called 'original sin,' (1) because it is derived from the original root of the human race; (2) because it is present in the life of every individual from the time of his birth, and, therefore, cannot be regarded as the result of imitation; and (3) because it is the inward root of all the actual sins that defile the life of man."[34]

Because of the Fall and suffering the consequence of original sin from the Fall, man now has a sinful nature that supposedly determines all he is and all he is able to do. Man, in this condition, is unable of—and many say incapable of—believing God or the gospel of Jesus Christ. We are said to be dead, blind, and deaf. Being born this way, man can only sin. He is utterly and totally incapable of doing anything that is good, spiritually or "supernaturally."[35]

As one scholar and teacher puts it, "We are not sinners because we sin. We sin because we are sinners."[36] This is the "total depravity" of man which in the words of Berkhoff, "indicates: (1) that the inherent corruption extends to every part of man's nature, to all the faculties and powers of both soul and body; and (2) that there is no spiritual good, that is, good in relation to God, in the sinner at all, but only perversion."[37]

When some Bible teachers try to soften the harsh evaluation of *total depravity* a bit by saying man is not as bad as he could be, they depend upon the presumption that God pours out restraining grace upon all, holding them back, so to speak, from completely manifesting their sinfulness. But this is no consolation or encouragement. Many believe God sees us as completely worthless because we are born as sinners as a result of Adam's and Eve's first sin. And even though we are not as bad as we could be, everything we do is bad, everything we do is sin. Since we cannot seek for God or respond to God in any way, we are in a hopeless situation. Or so our theological tradition tells us.

- If a mother nurses her newborn baby ... it is sin.
- If a stranger does something heroic and saves another person's life ... it is sin.
- If you care for a dying parent ... it is sin.
- If you help the homeless ... it is sin.

And by the way, since you are corrupt and can only sin, you deserve eternal separation from God. You deserve hell just for being born. This is not a stretch or a misunderstanding of what is being said in some theological circles. And this is what is taught in many churches.

Maybe you've heard it in your church.

Where do we come up with this stuff?

Does this fit the message of the Bible? Many think it does.

Does the Bible call man a sinner? Yes. Romans 3:23 says, "... for all have sinned and fall short of the glory of God." But to say "all sinned" is not the same as saying you are capable of nothing else but sin. To say all have sinned speaks to experience, not to identity.

Does this verse say sin is all we do or can do? No, it says this is a reality of the experience of all humans: we all sin. If I were to say, "All stay-at-home moms do laundry," this does not mean all stay-at-home moms *only* do laundry—even though it may feel like that to the stay-at-home mom. Surely, all stay-at-home moms do laundry, but that is not all they do, nor is it all they *can* do. It is certainly not who they are.

Romans 5:8 says, "But God demonstrates His own love toward us, in that while we were yet sinners, Christ died for us." Just because the people in the Roman church and Paul himself (he did write "we") sinned and, therefore, were sinners, doesn't mean sinning was all they did or could do. Nor does it mean this is who they were in their essence. When we commit personal sin, which every man will do in his life, we experience corruption and condemnation and can be rightly called a sinner. But even as a sinner with a principle of sin in our hearts (or a corrupt nature in our constitution), sin is not our only option. Not only did Paul do more than sin, he lived a righteous life unto the Lord *before* he accepted Jesus or His death on his behalf (Philippians 3:6). One sin could qualify a person for being described as a sinner, but he/she is much more because that is not all he/she can do. People do not have to obey the power of sin within them.

The parallel to this verse is found two verses prior where it says, "While we were still helpless,[38] at the right time, Christ died for the ungodly" (Romans 5:6). This means God did not wait until we got our act together to come and die for us. It means God put no conditions on us we had to meet to earn His love in Christ Jesus. It means God loved us even when we were rejecting Him and living in darkness. This must mean He still considers us significant and immeasurably valuable.

Possibly, the classic passage on man's supposed inability to live righteously is that of Paul when he wrote Romans 3:9-12:

> What then? Are we better than they? Not at all; for we have already charged that both Jews and Greeks are all under sin; as it is written, "There is none righteous, not even one; there is none who understands, there is none who seeks for God; all have turned aside, together they have become useless; there is none who does good, there is not even one.

Even if this is an accurate description of all of humanity (and contextually it is *only* a description of the two groups in the church at Rome, Jews and Gentiles, who were fighting with each other), it would be a description of experience and not capacity, of what they were presently doing—not a prescription of their nature or their ability. It certainly does not define man's intrinsic worth. And lest we miss Paul's point altogether, he is describing Christians here, not the supposed unbeliever who has not trusted in Jesus yet and is, therefore, doomed to hell.

Take for example the statement "none righteous" (Romans 3:10). Many people want us to believe this means man is not right; he is all wrong. Or, man is not right with God. But that is not what this means. When Paul says, "None [of you Roman Christians] are righteous," he is evaluating the spiritual state of the believers involved in the church split that was taking place over the Law in the life of the Christian. They were all responding in an ungodly fashion toward one another. He did not say that none of his addressees, who were all Christians, were capable of performing a righteous response to his brother in Christ. He is going to tell these same addressees in chapter six exactly how they can live righteously (Romans 6:16).

As another example, take the statement "none seek for God" (Romans 3:11). This does not say none *can* seek for God. This does not say man has lost his capacity to seek for God. This simply means none *are* seeking for God. It describes the Roman Christians' present experience, not their identity or capacity. They were fighting among each other over who would determine the standard by which the whole church would be accountable. None were seeking God and His will. All were trying to implement their own views.

On this note, when Paul was talking to the Athenians (Acts 17:27), he said God puts people in their particular places and times so that *"they should seek God*, if perhaps they might grope for Him *and find Him*, though He is not far off from each one of us" (italics mine).[39] That flies in the face of the idea we are so damaged in our humanity that we are incapable of seeking God. Actually, it affirms the exact opposite.

All the statements in Romans 3 that have been classically used to demolish the intrinsic worth of humanity do not speak to identity, intrinsic worth, or capacity. They relate the present experience of the Roman Christians to the past experience of God's chosen people, Israel. Both knew God and had a relationship with Him but were refusing to follow Him at the time they were being rebuked. There is a difference between Israel's *doing* and *being*, between the Roman Christians' *doing* and *being*, and our *doing* and our *being*.

We are talking apples and oranges.

Not Winning Friends

You must decide what makes sense in the text of the Bible. And what makes sense in your mind and your heart.

Most people think in order to reconcile people to God through Jesus Christ, the first and necessary step is to convince them how horribly rotten and damaged they are. What is worse is that to heighten this sense of their despicableness, the message also declares they deserve eternal damnation just for being born or for doing the least little sin. Most gospel presentations or tracts begin with this as the first step. This is illustrated clearly in the now well-known tract *The Roman Road to Salvation*. The first point: convince them they are a sinner deserving of hell.

So the first point in the "good news" is the *bad* news that we are all sinners deserving of eternal separation from God in a place called hell. But they don't just mean we are people who sin, we sin because we are sinners.[40] What they mean is that I have no other option; I am in complete subjection to sin and, therefore, deserving of damnation.

Lewis Smedes got the idea when he wrote:

> Grace felt heavy to me. The good news of grace only came after the bad news that I was mired in sin's clotted clay. I know now what the strategy was: the bad news meant to get me to feel so hopelessly flawed that I would be that much more grateful for the grace of God when it got to me. But, in fact, my spiritual malaise linked up with my chronic feeling of shame for being human, and the two of them brought forth in me a mess of homogenized shame. By the time the good word got to me, I was sunk so deep in my shame that I could feel no lightness in grace.[41]

People are not what they do. We are human beings, not human doings. We are created in the image of God. Do we sin? Yes. But to call someone a sinner as if this is their true identity is like viewing the world through a hole in the fence: your outlook is too small. Being a sinner may be a characterization of some, or even all, but it is not our intrinsic identity, nor does it delineate our sole capacity. Our hearts may become incorrigibly corrupt as a result of a lifetime of sinning, but we are not a slave to it unless we so choose to be.

Who am I? And do I deserve love and belonging? These are important questions in damning shame.

Man is essentially made in the image of God. He is intrinsically worthy, even if he has a nature that is receptive or susceptible to sin and chooses, thereby, to reject truth and walk in darkness. It is as a friend of mine wrote: "Even if the blackness should enshroud me for a lifetime, I am still worthy. Unchanged by the forces of this world, I am His beloved child. Worthy. Always worthy."[42] Man never loses his intrinsic value because of choices or lifestyle. Ron Allen writes, "In view of the Incarnation, the idea of man as a worm is mockery. In fact, to be truly human is to be majestic. *Worminess* is a distortion, not the ideal of the Creator."[43] As Allen continues, he writes that "The majesty of man is often hard to find east of Eden."[44] But it certainly is not impossible, as if man's value and majesty have ceased to exist. And to say man's capacity to respond to God has been lost is simply another way of saying man has been robbed of his intrinsic worth.

God holds us all accountable for trusting Him and walking with Him because we are capable of doing so. God desires for us to walk with Him because when we do, we experience life as it was intended by Him. In that walk, we will be blessed. So many people want to break man down to the lowest of lows because they think they are doing God a favor by emphasizing His sovereignty or exalting His grace. He has given us power and authority to choose Him, to choose life. And we can do it. In fact, that ability is taken for granted on every page of Scripture.

Ron Allen warns that the adverse "effects (of humanism) are incalculable" on our anthropology (the study of man). Allen writes:

> The main contributors to this humanistic and demeaned view
> of man are Copernicus who tried to marginalize man, Darwin
> who tried to reduce man to accident of matter, and Freud who
> tried to reduce man to subconscious impulses.[45]

All three have had a devastating effect on the majesty and worth of man. The church has joined the ranks and tried to make man worthless.

The message of the church has been: *You are no good; you are worthless, incapable of doing good, and incapable of seeking God.*

God's message to us is very different: You are capable and of incredible value and worth! Worth, not shame. Value, not garbage. This is what is right and true.

As a dear friend and mentor once wrote, "The proper study of man is not man; the proper study of man is God. Right living begins with right thinking. And right thinking begins with right thinking about God."[46]

God knows what we are worth.

I have a friend who makes his living and supports his family by selling stuff on eBay. He buys what others are selling at garage sales or on Craigslist, then turns around and sells it on eBay for more than he bought it—sometimes significantly more. The key to his success in this business is he knows what things are worth. When it comes to human value, only God knows what we are worth.

This reminds me of a poem titled, *The Dash*. Here are a couple of lines:

> I read of a man who stood to speak at the funeral of his friend.
> He referred to the dates on his tombstone from beginning …
> to the end.
> He noted that first came the date of his birth and spoke of the second with tears. But he said that what mattered most of all was the dash between those years.
> For that dash represents all the time that he spent alive on earth,
> And now only those who loved him know what that little line is worth.[47]

God loves you more than you will ever know, and He knows exactly what you are worth. You are worth everything that is most precious to Him. To deny our uniqueness and our awesomeness—just for being born—is to rob man of value and rob God of the praise He is worthy of as our Creator.

God says human beings are His workmanship (Ephesians 2:10). The Greek word for workmanship is *poiēma*, which is quite possibly where the word *poem* originated. It could be said that we human beings are masterpieces, works of art, songs to God, by God, and for God. We are His creative workmanship through which He communicates immeasurable worth. And I am sure you know how seriously creative persons take their creative expressions.

Finally, the most telling of all about who we are and how valuable we are to God is the story of the incarnation of the Son of God. That God would come to earth to become like us and do so in order to rescue us from sin and death, says very loudly and clearly that God values man. It says He loves us (John 3:16; 1 John 3:16; 4:10). It is not necessary to demean, diminish, or completely denigrate and destroy the object of His affection in order to bolster His affection. We don't need to make man scum to appreciate God's grace. God is love. The fact that He loved us enough to come and be one of us—and die for us—must mean He sees value and worth in us.

You are His creature and His beautiful poem that is, as yet, still unfinished.

Come out of the bushes.

God is speaking *to* you, and He has a lot He wants to say *through* you.

Now we consider death and deadness. Do those words really mean what they say?

---

27 A.W. Tozer, *A Journey Into the Father's Heart.*

28 http://rzim.org/just-a-thought-broadcasts/intrinsic-dignity.

29 Cain became angry; he was not always angry. His countenance had fallen, meaning it was not what it once was.

30 Many expositors of the Hebrew translate *elohim* as God, rather than following the LXX *aggellos.*

31 Ron Allen, *The Majesty of Man*, p. 77.

32 This is the idea behind the Hebrew word *palah*, which means to be separated or distinct. It is from the word *pala* which means to be surpassing, or extraordinary.

33 This is the idea behind the Hebrew word (*yare*) translated "fearfully." Something to be feared or revered and in awe of.

34 Berkhof, Louis, Systematic Theology, quoted from www.biblicaltraining.org.

35 Thomas Aquinas limited man's ability to doing "supernaturally good acts."

36 R.C. Sproul at http://www.ligonier.org/blog/tulip-and-reformed-theology-total-depravity/.

37 This is called "Common Grace."

38 In Greek *asthenēs means sick, or weak.*

39 Acts 17:27.

40 R.C. Sproul.

41 Lewis Smedes, *Shame & Grace*, p. 80.

42 Thanks to Sarah Van Diest for this one!

43 Ron Allen, *The Majesty of Man*, p.51.

44 Ron Allen; *The Majesty of Man*, p.103.

45 Ron Allen, *The Majesty of Man*, quoting Thielicke, p.28.

46 Earl D. Radmacher, *You & Your Thoughts; The Power of Right Thinking*, pp. 22, 28.

47 Linda Ellis, quoted from http://www.linda-ellis.com/the-dash-the-dash-poem-by-linda-ellis-.html.

Chapter 5
Zombie Killer

Born dead ... that is an oxymoron.
~ Anonymous

"You are dead to me!"

If you are a lover of mobster movies, you are as familiar with those words and their meaning as the nonverbal equivalent "the kiss of death." Mobsters take it to an extreme, literal end, but the intended meaning is this: the relationship is over—you're out of the family.

This phrase has been brought to primetime on the hit show *Shark Tank*. Often on the show when a budding entrepreneur with a great idea refuses the offer from billionaire shark-tank investor Kevin O'Leary, O'Leary brashly tells him, "You are dead to me." It is pretty obvious to all viewers exactly what Mr. O'Leary means when he utters these words.

Maybe you are a country music fan or a jilted lover like the one Dierks Bentley sings about in the song "You're Dead To Me."[48] It doesn't get more final than that. There certainly isn't the "let's still be friends" idea imbedded in those words. It's over. The meaning and intentions are obvious. The relationship we shared no longer exists because, in my mind, *you* do not exist. There is no hope for us—or for you.

Sadly, those are not just words spoken by Mafioso mobsters in Hollywood movies, by billionaire investors, or by country music stars. This path of harsh distancing and dissolution is all too common in our world, and the ones who have been shoved aside are left to struggle with the ensuing shame that comes from thinking they are not good enough. Not good enough for love. Not good enough for belonging. It is not that they have *done* wrong, but that they *are* wrong.

You may have been on the receiving end of such shunning. You may have heard someone you know say that to someone who had wronged or hurt them. It is the essence of one spouse saying to another, "I want a divorce." I've heard parents communicate this sentiment to their own children when they did not respect or obey them—even when the kids were grown adults at the time.

What is sad is that some people actually think this is a productive way to inspire others to be different or act differently. They called it "tough love," but it seems to be anything but. For many others, it is a means of manipulation. While that may occasionally work, it does not work all the time, or even most of the time. I agree with Brené Brown when she writes, "Worthiness is my birthright."[49] To take away a person's birthright is to rob him/her of his/her worthiness.

Ironically, the church has believed and taught the opposite. It has taught that we are unworthy at birth. Our birthright is that of the worthless and condemned.

Sadly, it seems most Christians have bought into this idea and, in fact, think it is necessary to adopt such a completely low view of man, of his ability to seek for God, and of his capacity to respond to God. How else can God's reputation (especially His sovereignty) be preserved? To require a person to hold on to these teachings as a way to inspire him to respond to God seems like some sort of reverse psychology at best: *You are dead, but if God comes calling, you had best respond.* You're dead, but you are responsible for your salvation—or at least accountable for it. This is the message the church needs to seriously reconsider and correct.

- Does the Bible really say we are unworthy just for being born?
- Does the Bible really reveal such a low view of man?
- Does God have such a low view of us? Are we dead to God?
- Are we really that worthless and incapable?
- Do we really have no birthright to any worth?

Original sin is the doctrine, as we have previously defined it, which teaches that all humanity fell sinful on the day Adam and Eve sinned and became depraved in nature: worthless, not able to do good, think good, or feel anything good. It is the idea that every person is born in sin, can only sin, and is born alienated from God and unable to seek for or respond to God. The traditional mantra states that when Adam sinned, being the head of the human race, all humanity was present in Adam, sinning with him. As a result, all men are, therefore, born sinners. All are dead to God. One pastor and author writes:

> The point of deadness is that we're incapable of any life with God. Our hearts were like a stone toward God (Ephesians 4:18; Ezekiel 36:26). Our hearts were blind and incapable of seeing the glory of God in Christ (2 Corinthians 4:4-6). We were totally unable to reform ourselves.[50]

- Incapable of any life with God.
- Hearts like stone toward God.
- Blind hearts, incapable of seeing God's glory.
- Totally unable to reform.
- We are totally depraved in our very essence and make-up.

Not only is that depressing, it is hard to obtain any worth from it, right?

We are taught: Since we are born dead "the sensibility to spiritual matters and the ability to act and respond spiritually, to do good things, are absent or severely impaired."[51] Since we are born dead and alienated from God, we can do no good and have no chance of relating to God without His intervention.

We are taught: We have been born with an evil disposition incapable of anything good. We are dead spiritually, and our *only* inclination is evil. Our actions are unspiritual, evil, and unrighteous because our "deadness to God" cannot allow any spirituality, goodness, or righteousness to be present or to be done by us. Sin is a matter of the entire person.[52] Even if we do something altruistically, it is nonetheless impure because we are dead. And most importantly, because all men are dead, they are "unable to extricate themselves from their sinful condition."[53] We are, according to one author, "totally unable and unwilling to seek God."[54] Or, as yet another author writes elsewhere:

> In summary, total depravity means that our rebellion against God is total; everything we do in this rebellion is sin, our

inability to submit to God or reform ourselves is total, and we are therefore totally deserving of eternal punishment.[55]

- Everything we do is sin.
- We are not able to submit to God.
- We deserve eternal punishment.
- We get all this just for being born.
- We've been robbed.

A.J. Swoboda tells of growing up along the Willamette River in Oregon and how he learned that sometimes when something looks dead, it is actually brimming with life beneath the surface. His words:

> Growing up in dark, drippy, soulful, Oregon winters, I'd watch the death of January conquer, year after year, the once free-flowing and wild Willamette River. By mid-month during the muffled silence of cold, a deep bone-chilling freeze would halt every living thing upon the face of our backyard. The Willamette fell victim with the rest. The river looked dead, frozen dead. But the frozen river wasn't really dead. My old man would tell me that underneath that cold, dark, seemingly dead surface was a wild, powerful primal flow which untrained eyes couldn't imagine. You had to *believe* it was alive. Rushing waves lurked underneath the stillness of death as powerful as ever. Dad knew it was there; below the surface. I believed it was there too. What appears as dead is really alive, alive like the wind … a primal flow secretly gushes on whether it's seen or not; below the surface, that is. Here's to seeing below the surface.[56]

Maybe we need to look beneath the surface. Maybe our theology has become like a thick layer of ice that conceals the life brimming below the surface. Is it possible we have completely misunderstood the capacity of man in favor of attempting to preserve God's sovereignty? Is it possible we have completely misunderstood death or being dead in the Bible? Is it possible there is life brimming below the surface, and all hope is not lost? Is it possible man's capacity is not the same thing as his experience?

Let's start back at the beginning and look below the surface. Upon a closer look, we might find that man is brimming with life, capability, and enormous possibilities. We should also find that God does not resemble a mafioso boss, egocentric billionaire investor, or a jilted lover. God never utters such brash, devastating, and harsh statements such as "You're dead to Me!" That fact alone should change our lives.

Once again, as we tested the idea of being damaged goods, let's test this theological premise that man is born dead. To do that correctly, we start back at the beginning.

Returning to the Garden

Back to Adam, Eve, the serpent, the fruit debacle, and to the death they died that day.

Let the story teach us. God told Adam and Eve, "... in the day that you eat from it, you will surely die" (Genesis 2:17). The serpent lied to them and said, "You surely will not die" (Genesis 3:4). God, who cannot lie (Numbers 23:19; Titus 1:2; Hebrews 6:18), must have been correct, and the day they ate, they died. So what was the nature of the death they died that day?

We can rule out both physical death as well as eternal death because, obviously, Adam and Eve did not die physically the day they ate the fruit, nor did an eternal death sentence get handed to them. (We will explore this more in the following chapter.)

The only option we are left with is *spiritual death.*

What is spiritual death? Is it holistic and all-encompassing? Is it instantaneous and momentary? Is spiritual death comprehensive? Does it describe a change in man's essence or his standing (position) with God? Did everything change? Or was their spiritual death a description of the moment? Was death momentary, conditional, and experiential, and not unconditional or unending? These are important questions.

Another important question is this: Is spiritual death how man *feels* toward God, how God relates to man, or both? When Jesus, in His humanity, cried out on the cross, "My God, My God, why have You forsaken Me?" (Matthew 27:46), is it possible Jesus *felt* separated when He took on our shame and bore the sins of the whole world?

Yet God the Father, on the other hand, did not actually separate from Him personally, for God would never leave Him or forsake Him (Deuteronomy 31:6; Hebrews 13:5). Is this not reasonable? Just a thought to ponder.

Let's go back to Genesis to test these ideas and answer these questions.

After Adam and Eve ate the fruit, they may have felt terrible about themselves, but that is not the impression given about how God felt or thought of them. Surely, it displeased God that they had disobeyed, but did God give them "the kiss of death" and say to them, "You're dead to Me"? Did God continue to pursue them?

When Adam and Eve ate the fruit from the tree of the knowledge of good and evil, they died *that day* just as God had warned (Genesis 2:17). The type of death they experienced was indicative of their experience of evil that brought shame, causing them to hide. They were estranged from the freedom and confidence they had prior to the illicit snack. They were estranged from God because they trusted in the snake (the mouthpiece of Satan) and were now serving his agenda rather than the one God gave them. And since a person cannot serve two masters at any given moment (same principle seen in Matthew 6:24), they were immediately experientially estranged from God. This is what we earn when we sin (Romans 6:23). They *experienced* evil. They did not instantaneously or comprehensively *become* evil.

They were hiding. They were separating themselves from God, having chosen evil.

Death is separation. But separation, in terms of our theological tradition, is given a finality that is not inherent or apparent in this story. Death is the interruption of relational experiences. God gives us a great picture of death in the story of the prodigal son. When the father is ready to party at the homecoming of the son, he says, "For this son of mine was dead, and has come to life again; he was lost and has been found" (Luke 15:24). Dead and lost, alive and found. The son had gone away to sow his wild oats, but the son was always a son. Both his deadness and lost-ness are descriptive of his experiences away from his father. They were the result of his choice to separate himself from his father. Obviously, the son was still alive, but he was not living. He was unproductive because he disconnected himself from his true identity/life. He was living but dead, unproductive and depriving himself—even when he thought he was living it up.

The final verses of the story of the prodigal son (Luke 15:31-32) are phenomenal and very telling. First, the father says to the older son, "Son, you have always been with me, and all that is mine is yours." This older son was never separated from the father or his resources. This older son never deprived himself of all that life was and could be by choosing to walk away/apart from the father. Then the father says, "For this brother of yours was dead and has begun to live; and was lost and has been found" (Luke 15:32). The younger son never lost his identity but had lost his way. In returning, he began to live again; he found himself.

The son was *dead* and *lost* in the sense of disappearing and hiding. When he returned to his father, he was described as *alive* and *found*. Despite the change in circumstances, there was no change in position or standing in the family. So the fact remains: the prodigal was still related to the elder brother as "his brother" and to the father as "this son of mine." Disappearing or hiding is not living in relationship. And that kind of living is actually depriving oneself of the core blessing in life.

That is the nature of the death we see Adam and Eve experiencing the day they ate.

The fruit was from the tree of the knowledge of good and evil, yet knowledge can be more than data in the mind. It can be a type of experience, an experiential knowledge. So, is it possible that when they trusted the serpent and ate the fruit, the experience itself was the opposite of life (death)?

The Bible says, "Then the eyes of both of them were opened, and they knew they were naked; and they sewed fig leaves together and made themselves loin coverings" (Genesis 3:7). The nakedness itself was not evil since they were previously "naked and not ashamed" (Genesis 2:25), but what was once good became distorted in their experience of death. They were, for the very first time, experiencing disobedience and (knowing) evil. This is death.

The experience of evil is death. Evil, by its very nature, is distinct from God, who is light and good and love. They disobeyed God. They rejected God, and they trusted the serpent. As they walked in evil, they experienced death. They separated themselves from God and from their own created goodness and purpose. But that separation was in the moment of disobedience and does not describe a *fall* from their essential relationship with God as a family member. Their relationship with God was not lost. Their separation did not describe some change in their capability to respond to God. Their separation was strange since it was contrary to God and how they were created to live. Their separation was estrangement; they were living like strangers, although they knew each other well.

We, like Adam and Eve, become slaves to the one we choose to obey. This is why we cannot serve two masters at any given moment. If we enslave ourselves to one master, we are detached or estranged from the other. When we choose to walk the path of death, even if it seems right to us (see Proverbs 14:12), we are strangers to life and God. It is not that God does not know us or that we have no knowledge of God, but we live as practical atheists (in Ephesians 2:12 "without God" is *atheoi* in Greek). So we are "excluded" or "alienated" (same word in Greek: *apallutrioō*), which means we are not belonging to God or we are living as strangers (*allotrios* means belonging to another, so *apallutrioō* is away from belonging to another: estranged). The reason for this estrangement is not in God but in man, "because of the ignorance that is in them, because of the hardness of their heart" (Ephesians 4:18). Or, as in Colossians 1:21, "formerly alienated and hostile in mind, engaged in evil deeds..." It is the experience that is estranged. It is also very strange because this is not how we are created to live, nor is it God's desire for us.

Back to Adam and Eve. Despite their choice to sin, their capacity to respond to God did not change when they were escorted out of the Garden or when they had children. And it did not change the capacity of their children or their children's children.

Life after the Fall became like a road with two lanes or two paths. Just because a person chooses to walk one path does not mean he does not have the capability to walk the other path. When a person walks the wrong path, or maybe better said that he *chooses* to walk toward death instead of toward life, it describes his experience, not his essence. It is *being* versus *doing* again, capability versus experience.

And then Adam and Eve had children.

Sadly, we know how the story goes. Cain does not choose to trust God, and he does not master sin. Cain killed his brother. He did the work of the evil one (1 John 3:12) as his parents had done before him. This is a result of choices, not capacity or capability. Cain's murderous way was a result of his choice and describes his experience, not his essence nor his human constitution or capacity. He is a descendant of Adam, just like all those born in Adam. Cain was sent east of Eden. He was cursed from the ground and made to be a vagrant and wanderer (Genesis 4:11-12). Cain went out from the "face of the Lord" (Genesis 4:16), yet he went with God's provision and protection (Genesis 4:15). To say Cain was eternally separated from God or completely severed from God is to go way beyond what the text of the Bible offers.

Not everyone chooses the path Cain chose. Some actually seek God. Some call on God (Genesis 4:26), some walk with God (Genesis 5:22), and some have evil hearts and do evil continually (Genesis 6:5). Others are righteous (Genesis 6:9).

Obviously, man has the power to do evil and to do what is right. Man has the capacity to deny God and the capacity to respond to God. This premise can be proven throughout the entire Old Testament. So where do we come up with this idea that depravity and deadness refer to being totally severed from God and without the capability of responding to God?

As I mentioned before, we have a tendency to bring our preconceived beliefs into our Bible reading instead of allowing the words on the pages to speak for themselves. I think that's what has happened here.

Rhyme and Reason

There is an old English rhyme that brides carry forward in modern day wedding celebrations: "Something Olde, Something New, Something Borrowed, Something Blue, A Sixpence in your Shoe."[57] The old represents continuity. The new represents optimism for the future.

The borrowed is for shared happiness. Blue is for love, purity, and fidelity while the sixpence in the shoe is to call a cab if you think you made a mistake ... just kidding! The New Testament is an application and fulfillment of the Old Testament. There is very little that is new. There is plenty that is borrowed and plenty that is blue. The message is completely continuous from the Old Testament to New Testament: a story about future hope and prosperity. There is absolute rhyme and reason from the Old Testament to the New Testament. So let's take what we learned from the Old and see how it fits the New. If clear indication is given that something else, something new, is meant, we will receive that as progressive truth revealed by God.

Let's start in Ephesians 2:1-3 where we read:

> And you were dead in your trespasses and sins, in which you formerly walked according to the course of this world; according to the prince of the power of the air, of the spirit that is now working in the sons of disobedience. Among them we too all formerly lived in the lusts of our flesh, indulging in the desires of the flesh and of the mind, and were by nature children of wrath, even as the rest.

Here is what some write about this verse. We can begin to see where the idea of depravity and deadness may arise:

> We emerge from the womb wholly inclined to break God's law. In sum, we are dead upon arrival into this world, spiritually speaking, and we hate God, the Lord and giver of true life ... we are born dead ... even though we have the power to choose, we are dead to the things of God, and as a result we have no desire for the things of God. Rather, we follow a different course. We follow it willfully; we follow it freely, in the sense of doing what we want to do. But with respect to spiritual things, we are dead.[58]

Therefore, according to some, because I am born dead in my trespasses and sins, I am unable to have any positive response to or relationship with God. I don't have the capacity in and of myself to respond to God or to even want a relationship with Him. My capability to seek Him is completely and utterly non-existent. I am dead upon arrival. I am born dead.

Read those verses again. Do they really say all this author claims?

Are the verses describing the condition in which a person is born? Or are they describing the way people walk? The practical understanding is only reinforced by the statement connected to this in verse 2, which states "in which you formerly walked." The emphasis is on walking and, therefore, is looking at experience, not position or constitution. They are not describing how or in what state a person is born into this world.

Was Cain born dead or did Cain experience death as he chose to walk in trespasses and sins? Are these verses in Ephesians describing essence or experience? There is a huge difference. We should remember how important it is for us to maintain the distinction between *doing* and *being*, between *experience* and *essence*. Our sense of worth or shame hangs in the balance.

Paul says the people he was writing to ("you") were dead in trespasses and sins, in which they walked according to the course of this world. The deadness was their resultant experience as they walked "in trespasses and sins." This statement is not positional or about man's intrinsic worth. This is about his practice or experience. When the Ephesians were previously sinning, they were walking according to the course of this world and were dead. That is, they were experiencing death as they walked. One could say they were walking in death and away from God by the choices they were making.

Paul is not saying death and sin were the only possible experiences available to them. The verse does not say they were born dead. Deadness relates to the experience of trespasses and sins. This eliminates (or reduces) the possibility of interpreting this as a description of man's nature or essence. The previously quoted author misses that distinction when he writes, "To be dead to sin is to be in a state of moral and spiritual bondage. By nature we are slaves to sin."[59] And as another theologian writes, "Now it will surely be admitted that to be dead, and to be dead in sin, is clear and positive evidence that there is neither aptitude nor power remaining for the performance of any spiritual action."[60]

That jump is way too far.

The experience of sin, and, therefore, deadness, does not assume that power or aptitude for something better is void or nonexistent. We don't need to jump that far. We don't need to destroy man's intrinsic worth so completely.

If the passage is to be understood in a practical sense, it would then mean the people to whom Paul is writing in the church at Ephesus were *dead as they trespassed and sinned*. The same can and should be said for any person: If you walk in sin, you experience deadness—a death just like Adam experienced in the Garden of Eden. One just like Cain. One just like those who died in the flood and so on. As Adam and Eve walked in trespasses and sins, when they trusted the serpent and ate the fruit, they experienced death. Every human being who chooses to sin is dead in the sphere of that experience. But there is life brimming below the surface.

This death is a universal experience of all men because all sin. When Paul wrote to the Roman church, he penned these words, "Therefore, just as through one man sin entered into the world, and death through sin, and so death spread to all men, because all sinned" (Romans 5:12).

A similar statement is made in Romans 5:17: "For if by the transgression of the one, death reigned through the one…" And again in Romans 5:21 where we read, "…sin reigned in death…"

Death did spread to all men because when any man sins, he experiences the domain of darkness and death. Sin is a dominating force in this world, and our bodies are susceptible to its temptations. But we do not have to obey it.

We can be slaves to sin, but you are only a slave to the one whom you choose to obey (Romans 6:16). Adam and Eve obeyed the serpent, and they sinned. They became, in that moment, a slave to sin. When the generations that came after Adam and Eve fell prey to some temptation to sin, it could be said of them that thereafter, each person had the potential of living life in a way that "every intent of the thoughts of his heart was only evil continually" (Genesis 6:5). But this only describes the historical situation being discussed and does not intend to say something about the necessary limitations of the constitution of all of humanity born of Adam.

If the latter were true, how would we explain the fact that Noah, who was "a righteous man, blameless in his time," walked with God (Genesis 6:9)?

To say that because the Bible tells us "the intent of man's heart is evil from his youth" (Genesis 8:21), man is, therefore, void of life and the capacity to do good, is to read more into the verse than Moses meant to communicate. To misunderstand and misuse a verse in ways such as this ultimately devastates and robs man of his intrinsic value and worth. Man, in his fallen state, may be inclined to evil, but that is not who he is or all he can do. These sorts of pregnant interpretations destroy the very fabric of our intrinsic value and worth, thus mounding on our heads heaping piles of manure called shame. And that stinks.

When any person chooses to serve Satan or sin, they experience evil. The nature of that path is death, a separation from God and all that is good. When any person chooses that path, they are naturally hostile to God and become an enemy of God—experientially, but not constitutionally. I am dead when I walk in sin (evil) but when I am not sinning, would it not be safe to assume I am not dead? God makes alive any and all who look to Him by faith, regardless of the time/period or place in which they live.

In Paul's words to the Ephesians (2:5), "But God … even when we were dead in our transgressions, made us alive together with Christ (by grace you have been saved), and raised us up with Him …" This is what God has been doing and will continue to do for all who look to Him and choose to walk the path of life, not death.

Zombies

Someone once said the idea of man's total depravity and deadness is like a zombie—the living dead. Zombies, they went on to explain, are deteriorating and putrefying. But wait just one second; zombies are not real. Boom!

We are not zombies. We are not rotting flesh. Just because we are dead when we sin doesn't mean we are only dead or that we can only sin. Is it really necessary for man to have such a low view of himself in order to bring him to walk with God by faith? Is it more inspiring to tell people they can't do it, or could it be more inspiring to tell people they can?

I know that when I talk to my two sons about their futures, I want them to believe they can do anything they put their minds to. I don't think it will help in the long run if I degrade them and tell them they can't do this or that. I fear that if I did destroy their sense of worth in this way, they might live with me forever and stay in their rooms and play video games—zombie-killer video games no less. Of course, when I tell them they can do anything, I add that with God's help, nothing is impossible. I want them to take their capacity and unite it to God's life through the person of Jesus Christ, through whom they can do all things (Philippians 4:13).

- We *can* seek God.
- We *can* respond to God.
- We *can* exercise faith.
- We are *not* incapacitated.
- We have a birthright to worth.

Not everyone will seek God or respond to Him every time. But we are capable. We have the capacity.

This is why Paul could tell the Athenians that God "made from one, every nation of mankind to live on the face of the earth, having determined their appointed times, and the boundaries of their habitation, that they should seek God, if perhaps they might grope for Him and find Him, though He is not far off from each one of us."

Look up. God is not far off. Seek. Grope. Find.

There is life brimming below the surface.

---

48 Dierks Bentley, "Up On the Ridge," Capitol Records, 2010.

49 Brené Brown, *Daring Greatly*, p.169.

50 John Piper, *Five Points*, p. 22.

51 Millard J. Erickson, *Christian Theology*, p.614.

52 Ibid, p.628.

53 Ibid, p.630.

54 John F. MacArthur, Jr., *The Gospel According to Jesus*, p.92.

55 John Piper, quoted from http://www.desiringgod.org/articles/what-we-believe-about-the-five-points-of-calvinism#Depravity.

56 A.J. Swoboda, *A Glorious Dark*, pp. 1-2.

57 Quoted from https://en.wikipedia.org/wiki/Something_old.

58 R.C. Sproul, quoted from www.ligonier.org/learn/devotionals/dead-arrival.

59 R.C. Sproul, *Grace Unknown*, p.130.

60 Loraine Boettner, *Predestination*, pp.65-66.

Chapter 6
Damned or Not?
Damn Damnation

If you are going through hell, keep on going.[61]
~ Winston Churchill

Born damaged, born dead. Or so they say.

But worse even yet: born *DAMNED*!

Many people genuinely believe every single human being ever born is born deserving eternal damnation in a place called hell. Some negotiate around the harshness of such an idea by suggesting there must be an "age of accountability," which would mean babies and toddlers are innocent. Yet, if they make it past a certain age, the sentence of hell is slapped on them just because they are human. By "that age," the experts say, they will have certainly sinned knowingly and willfully.

This is not an opinion shared by all, but at least it recognizes the problem with the traditional view. What the majority of scholars and teachers of the traditional view believe is that everyone born is born damned. It may be a belief you grew up with or were taught somewhere along the way. It may be an idea you have accepted as true. What does this teaching say about our intrinsic worth? What effects can this belief have on our experience of shame?

Just to bring it home, think about it this way. When you visit a mother and newborn baby in the hospital and you look at the newborn, you might say (or think) something like:

- Oh, what a bundle of joy.
- She is so precious, so cute.
- A wonder of life.
- A special gift from God.

But if you were thinking theologically, you might *think* (because no one would dare *say* such a thing): *She is such a cutie. Too bad she's going to hell.*

Sounds silly to think in these terms, but this is exactly the theological premise behind the vast majority of Christian teaching and belief. This is how most people view God and how most believe God thinks about them. But is this really what the Bible says?

Does the Bible say the God who creates life does so with a sentence of eternal damnation hanging over every single baby ever born?

Have you ever wrestled with this issue? Have you tested this belief against Scripture?

This is a life and death issue. This is another central issue of errant beliefs that directly or indirectly causes shame. Remember, we get our sense of intrinsic worth from God as the source of absolute truth and goodness. When we have errant beliefs about God or the way we think God views us, those beliefs become a source of shame and rob us of our essential worth.

Maybe you have never struggled with this issue, or maybe you just ignored the uneasy feelings when the subject came up. Most have run into others who struggle with this subject. Many reject the idea on a purely emotional basis while some are afraid to even question the topic for fear of criticism or condemnation. Many struggle intensely with what their Christian faith *supposedly* says about them. To be born with such deficit? To start off in life so far behind? It reminds me of stories on the news or in the paper, where a newborn child was found in a trash bag in the dumpster of Taco Bell. It doesn't seem fair ... or right!

Has anyone ever come to you who was struggling with this issue? What did you do? Did you encourage them to embrace their doubt and question the premise? Did you encourage them to open the Bible to test it? Or did you shush them and tell them not to go there? In your own mind, you don't want to go there, and neither should they. But life forces us to go there. We must face these issues and beliefs head on. Burying our heads in the sand or hiding in the bushes is exactly what God's adversary, the Devil, wants us to do. The Devil twists the word of God so subtly, but severely, that God becomes unrecognizable. The god we think we see is so scary that we are off to the bushes just like Adam, hiding in shame.

As hard as it is to think through this issue, this is important stuff to reconsider. Because—if this is true—a baby lying in a crib is destined to hell for being born in the likeness of Adam. If this is true, a two-year-old toddler playing in the mud deserves eternal torment and God's wrath because all he can do is sin. Even his playing in the mud is sin and deserving damnation.

This issue of damnation is central to what so many call the "good news," but is this really *good* news?

When we talk about hell or damnation theologically, we mean what most mean: the punishment of eternal damnation, experiencing God's wrath forever. Hell is a place of unending duration of punishment and torment. Damnation usually refers to that punishment.

Recall the quote from chapter five: "Total depravity means that our rebellion against God is total, everything we do in this rebellion is sin, our inability to submit to God or reform ourselves is total, and we are therefore totally deserving of eternal punishment."[62] We are, according to that writer, born totally depraved and deserving of damnation. Those who don't meet this fate, the scholars surmise, are spared because of God's great grace and mercy to choose them for heaven while all others get what they deserve. It is not a pretty picture. As one author puts it:

> Hell is an eternity before the righteous, ever-burning wrath of God. A suffering torment from which there is no escape and no relief.[63]

This is a dreadful reality for many if not most of humanity. The same author writes:

> If we try to imagine the worst of all possible suffering in the here and now, we have not yet stretched our imaginations to reach the dreadful reality of hell ... there is no biblical concept more grim or terror-invoking than the idea of hell.[64]

On one piece of this, many people agree: dreadful and terror-invoking. But biblical?

If this is true, then it ought to be clear and explicit in the Bible. If it is true, then it must reasonably harmonize with the reality that God is love, and He loves the whole world (John 3:16). But does it?

Dante pictured hell as nine concentric circles.[65] Milton wrote that it is one great furnace.[66] Bosch depicted hell as a place of demonic torture.[67] Many medieval artists paint hell engulfed in flames to depict its violent ethos. Sartre said hell is other people.[68] Aldous Huxley said this earth could be another planet's hell.[69] George Bernard Shaw said that a perpetual holiday was hell.[70] Our concern is not with Dante, Milton, Bosch, Michelangelo, or Jean-Paul Sartre. Our concern is what the Bible says. What does the Bible say hell is? Where is it? Who goes there and why? For how long? For what purpose? Our concern is whether hell—as a place of eternal punishment just for being born—is even biblical. Our concern is whether or not the Bible says hell is the deserved destination for every human being born in the likeness of Adam.

Since we are testing an ideology, let us begin with a reasonable premise to test. If hell is the deserved punishment of eternal separation from God to experience His wrath, it is reasonable and logical to assume that God would make this clear and explicit. Such important and significant truths *ought* to be clear and explicit. Damnation just for being born *ought* to be clear and explicit. That is a fair premise to be tested.

From Front to Back

Traditional Christian teaching indicates that the consequence of damnation originated with Adam, so we should expect this to be clearly revealed and explicitly stated in Genesis and/or somewhere in the Old Testament. This should be true before we move forward to other verses that pick up on Adam's story or elaborate on the meaning of his story.

So what do we see in our reading of the early chapters of Genesis? This may surprise you.

When you read the opening chapters of Genesis, what you do *not* find is God warning Adam and Eve they will go to hell when and if they disobey Him, or when and if they ever sin. Neither will you find in Genesis, anything about God giving some indication that as a result of sin, Adam and Eve would now be hell bound. You will not find any indication that Adam and Eve's descendants would be damned to hell just for being born in their likeness.

When God warned Adam and Eve, He said:

> But from the tree of the knowledge of good and evil you shall not eat, for in the day that you eat from it you shall surely die. (Genesis 2:17)

You eat, you die. Death is the consequence of disobeying God. That is a clear statement. Death is the forewarned immediate consequence of eating from the tree of the knowledge of good and evil. God did not say He would kill them, but that death would be indicative if they ate. There is nothing here about hell or eternal torment as a consequence of sin. There is nothing explicitly stated that would indicate the "death" God warned about was *eternal* death, *eternal* torment, or hell. In fact, it is not in any way clear that this death had anything to do with man's eternal destiny. At best, the only thing many authors, teachers, and scholars offer is to say that hell as Adam and Eve's destiny is *implied* in the story. Implication, in my opinion, is not good enough for such a serious matter as this. In reality, the only way it is even implied is if the reader had gained understanding from some other source and brought it with them to their reading of Genesis. To suggest that something is implied is to admit the idea in question is not actually to be found in the text.

Since the idea of eternal death is not in the text itself, we have no reason to put it there by reading it into the story.

Nothing in the story gives us any indication that relationship with God was lost or severed completely or eternally. Their relationship to God—and God's commitment to them—were still very much intact. This is the story of the first sin, the Fall.

What about *the curse*? If ever there would be a good place for God to reveal such serious eternal ramifications of sin, this would be the place. What we find from reading Genesis 3:14-19 is that while the serpent was cursed (3:14) and the land was cursed (3:17), the man and the woman were not cursed. Adam and Eve received consequences—pain in childbirth and toil on the earth—but no *curse*. Also, we must limit how far we push the meaning of words like *curse* since the curses given in Genesis 3 are temporal and not eternal. You can read this on your own and see how plainly this is based on what is said. What is obvious is that eternal damnation is neither clear nor explicit, nor is it even implied.

So we read on.

In Genesis 3:23-24, we read that one of the changes taking place as a result of Adam and Eve's sin was that they were removed from the Garden of Eden. The stated (clear and explicit) purpose for their removal was so they would not eat of the tree of life and live forever (Genesis 3:22). This means Adam and Eve would not live forever in their earthly existence; their bodies would return to dust (Genesis 3:19). This has to do with their physical life (mortal), not their immortal soul (Ecclesiastes 12:7). There is nothing clear, explicit, or implied that a sentence of eternal damnation was to be realized once they died physically. Nor do you get the idea that their relationship with Yahweh had been severed or lost temporarily or eternally, for God went with them east of the Garden (Genesis 4). There is nothing clear and explicit about eternal damnation or hell. And so on we read, from front to back.

You could read on and on through the Old Testament, and you wouldn't find any sentence of eternal condemnation. No mention of hell anywhere. You won't read about it in Genesis 4 in the story of Adam and Eve's first descendants. In fact, you won't find it anywhere in the Pentateuch (the first five books of the Bible) written by Moses.

Don't you think that if God instructed Moses to write the Pentateuch (Genesis, Exodus, Leviticus, Numbers, and Deuteronomy) to teach the nation of Israel how to live rightly before Him, it would be safe to assume God would make something that serious—the possible experience of hell for eternity—clear? We would also expect a solution to remedy the possible experience of such a severe state to be clear, wouldn't we? But it is not. Not in the Ten Commandments, and not in any of the 613 Laws of the Mosaic Covenant. Nothing. Nada. Zilch.

You will have to keep reading a long time before you come upon a passage in the Old Testament that could even possibly be twisted and contorted to refer to such a dastardly thing.

Where is Hell in the Old Testament?

Some might drag you to Daniel 12:2 to support their idea that eternal damnation is a real and deserving punishment for the wicked in the Old Testament:

> Now at that time, Michael, the great prince who stands over the sons of your people, will arise. And there will be a time of distress such as never occurred since there was a nation until that time; and at that time your people, everyone who is found written in the book, will be rescued. And many of those who sleep in the dust of the ground will awake, these to everlasting life, but the others to disgrace and everlasting contempt.

But wait a second; Daniel is a book with a mix of history and prophecy that came to the prophet during the Babylonian exile of the nation of Israel. Daniel's prophecies are about the fall of human-led kingdoms and the establishment of God's kingdom—the coming kingdom of Messiah—on this earth (see Daniel 2:44). The prophetic promises to the nation of Israel are about God's plan for future restoration—prophecies about how God will crush the kingdoms of this world and establish His kingdom, the kingdom of Messiah (Daniel 2:31-45; 7:13; 9:24-27) upon this earth.

In Daniel, "everlasting life" and "everlasting contempt" are long durations of good or chastisement that will be realized during that coming kingdom. These are not about eternity as in outside of time and unending in duration. It might be a bit confusing because of the use of the word *everlasting*. But there was no word in either Hebrew, or biblical Greek for that matter, which directly corresponds to our English word *eternal* (as in beyond time, after time, or unending duration). The idea behind the Hebrew word *olam* is an indescribable long duration of time. It is like saying that while I am waiting for my food at the fast-food counter, "This food is taking *forever*." I don't mean forever in the sense of a literal eternity. I am saying it is taking an inordinate amount of time—a whole lot longer than I anticipated or imagined.

The "everlasting life" of Daniel 12:2 is a synonym for Messiah's kingdom that is being promised to the nation who will inherit it (Daniel 7:18; 12:13). The judgment (disgrace and everlasting contempt) corresponds and is contrasted with the reward of that life.

When Jesus spoke to the rich young ruler (Matthew 19:16-29) who came to Him asking how he could obtain eternal life (Matthew 19:16), it is not a stretch to think this rich young Jew could have had Daniel 12:1-2 in mind when he made his request. Eternal life is clearly a synonym for the earthly kingdom since Jesus seamlessly changes between the phrase eternal life and kingdom in His dialogue with the young ruler (Matthew 19:16, 23, 24, 29).

The bottom line is that the idea of eternal torment in a place called hell is not what is behind the prophecy of Daniel. The big cash-out is this: The concept of eternal damnation is noticeably absent in Genesis and in Exodus, Leviticus, Numbers, Deuteronomy, and every other book in the Old Testament. This might explain why most Jewish people have no concept of hell or eternal damnation—as Christians understand it—in their orthodoxy.

Hell is not an Old Testament teaching.

New Testament on Hell?

So that leaves us with an important question. Does the New Testament teach the idea that we are born deserving eternal damnation? If so, then it is understandable how people miraculously find the idea in the Old Testament. But what if our understanding is wrong? What if there is a better way to interpret and understand the New Testament?

Take, for example, Romans 5:12. There we read, "Just as through one man sin entered into the world, and death through sin, and so death spread to all men, because all sinned." Let's simplify this verse. Here are the statements:

- Sin entered into the world through one man: Adam.
- Death entered through sin.
- Death spread to all men because all men sinned.

Same premise as before. Is there anything here that might change the way we read and understand Genesis? What is clear is that death came as a result of sin. What is not clear is the meaning of death. It does not clearly say anything like eternal death, spiritual death, or physical death. So we go back to the original story and ask, "What death did Adam experience when he sinned?" The death Adam experienced is the same death all men experience when they turn away from God and sin. This death is, as Paul states elsewhere, the "wages of sin" (Romans 6:23) and will result in personal or particular sins carried out in death (Romans 5:20-21).

To make this death synonymous with eternal death or damnation is to make it say more than Paul ever intended, and certainly more than is clear and explicit. And most importantly, to identify death as eternal punishment would directly contradict the reading of the historical account in Genesis. The death that came as a result of Adam's sin spread to all men because it is a universal experience (consequence) of sin. When we sin, we die just like Adam and Eve did when they disobeyed. This death is spiritual and describes our experience, not our essence.

There is great debate as to the nature of the flesh, which some call our "sin nature," and what the Bible calls the body of sin (Romans 6:6). To be dogmatic about what sin is—an entity, a physiological thing, or a propensity—is unnecessary and something the Bible does not define. Sin is not my nature, although it does have the capacity to reign by making the members of my body its servant. Sin is not my only option. I have to go down the path before God gives me over (Romans 1:24, 26, 28). Whether sin is an external force and becomes an internal reality (taking up residence) when man submits the members of his body, or is an internal propensity or principle called "indwelling sin," what is true is that now all who are born from Adam are subject to sin's desire to usurp and dominate. But that does not mean this is our only option.

We read in Romans 5:16, 18, "The gift is not like that which came through the one who sinned; for on the one hand the judgment arose from one transgression resulting in condemnation ... So then as through one transgression, there resulted condemnation to all men, even so through one act of righteousness there resulted justification of life to all men."

These verses give much of the same information as verse 12 but in a slightly different way. Here are the important statements to consider:

- Judgment arose from one transgression.
- Condemnation for all men resulted from the one transgression because all sin.

It is not the one sin of Adam but the one sin that all men commit (Romans 5:12-13). When I sin, the condemnation comes upon me. The condemnation is the negative propensity to turn away from God and obey sin that indwells me. I do not have to follow sin. It is a lord when it rules me, but I have other options. Sin does not have to rule me.

God cannot accept intimate fellowship with any who choose to act independently and turn away from Him. He can still love us even while He rejects or condemns actions that result in death. This death has nothing to do with man's capacity to respond to God. It can be overcome by trusting God. But as it was with Cain, the same is true for anyone born in the likeness of Adam: we don't have to serve sin. We can master it by God's grace, through faith.

Condemnation is the consequence of sin, which leads to further propensity to allow sin to be our master. The condemnation is not eternal condemnation. When we sin—and we all do at one time or another—we experience this consequence of sin's presence. Regardless of what one decides on sin's presence—internal (a part of our nature) or external (an outside influence)—sin's presence does not mean it has absolute power as if it is the only option man has. Jesus came to condemn sin in the flesh (Romans 8:3) and by His Spirit to set us "free from the law of sin and death" (Romans 8:2).

It is the decision of man to turn away from God and serve sin, upon which the wrath of God is presently being revealed (see Romans 1:18).

A Word on Wrath

Living under an errant belief of God will lead quickly and naturally to a life of shame. One such belief that fans the flames of shame is misunderstanding God's wrath. The Bible has much to say about God's wrath and how He punishes those who sin. There are many stories and verses in both Old and New Testaments that speak of His wrath being poured out upon the earth and mankind. What is a wrong assumption to make, however, is that His wrath is eternal in nature or lays a sentence of eternal damnation upon the sinner.

It is not safe or correct to assume that when God acts in His wrath to chastise those who sin—even if the chastisement is physical death—His temporal punishment of death leads to eternal punishment in hell.

God's wrath has been and always will be temporal.

Read that one again. *God's wrath has been and always will be temporal,* as in limited duration and within time. Temporary.

God's wrath is NOT eternal.

Never do we find any statement in the Bible, the *whole* Bible, which says God's wrath is eternal. Not one verse. In fact, the opposite is clearly revealed.

David sang of the temporal nature of God's anger/wrath when he penned the words of Psalm 30:4-5: "… give thanks to His holy name, for His anger is but for a moment, His favor is for a lifetime; weeping may last for the night, but a shout of joy comes in the morning."

In Psalm 103:9 we read that God will not keep His anger forever, while the lovingkindness of the Lord is everlasting (Psalm 103:17). In Isaiah 26:20 we read that the indignation of God has its course in time and will run its course for the purpose for which God expresses it in time. And—possibly most telling—we are told "the wrath of God is finished" in the pouring out of the seven last plagues in the second half of the Tribulation (Revelation 15:1).

When people talk about disciplining their children, some say you should not do so in anger. If by anger they mean rage and lack of self-control, we should all agree with this prohibition. However, if by anger they mean indignation over a wrong done, then when else would you discipline your children? When parents discipline, they are operating in wrath. God's wrath and anger are God's righteous indignation. Of course He is angry when we do wrong because He knows sin is not good for us. It is evil, brings death, and does not bring Him glory. But His wrath and anger cannot exist apart from His loving nature, so His wrath and anger are righteous and loving; they represent a righteous indignation that flows from holy love and is for our good. He loves us. Therefore, He will discipline us when we do wrong.

Back to hell, or to hell and back. Let's move on to see what Jesus has to say about the subject of hell.

Huios (Son) on Hell

I have heard and read numerous times that Jesus spoke more about hell than any other subject. I have heard the same about money. I guess it depends on what the preacher is driving home that particular Sunday. I believe this is a serious misunderstanding to say Jesus spoke more about hell than any other subject because Jesus never spoke about hell, except four times in His revelation to John where it is called the "lake of fire, the second death" (Revelation 2:11, 20:10, 14-15; 21:8). Four times. Apart from that, never.

Where does all the confusion about Jesus and hell stem from? The misunderstanding comes from an unfortunate English translation of the Greek word *Gehenna*. The NASB and the NIV have thirteen uses in the New Testament of the English word *hell*. Eleven of the thirteen are translations of *Gehenna* found in the gospels, reported to have come from the lips of Jesus. Opinions vary widely on the meaning of *Gehenna*, but there is strong biblical evidence that should clear up any confusion and misunderstanding.

The historical understanding of *Gehenna* comes from the Hebrew Scriptures, what most Christians call the Old Testament. The evidence in the Hebrew Scriptures is strong and more than sufficient to develop our understanding. If we rely on the inspired Word of God (2 Timothy 3:16), any extra-biblical, historical, or archeological studies are secondary, at best, and prove unnecessary in the end.

Gehenna is the Greek word derived from the Hebrew name for the *Wadier-Rababai,* otherwise known in Hebrew as *Ge-Hinnom,* which means the valley of Hinnom, a ravine south of Jerusalem.[71] The first mention of this geographical site is in Joshua 15:7 where it is a border reference of Judah's portion of the Promised Land. In Joshua 18:16 it is used similarly as a border to Benjamin's portion of the land. It is used again as a geographical reference in Nehemiah 11:30. These references are purely geographical and theologically benign.

The next time we find the valley of Ge-Hinnom, it is anything but benign. It is absolutely malignant and bursting with significance. Under the leadership of King Ahaz (2 Chronicles 28:1-4; 2 Kings 16:1-4) and later King Manasseh (2 Chronicles 33:1-6; 2 Kings 21:1-9), both wicked kings were reported to have done evil in the sight of the Lord. Both wicked kings erected altars to Baal, practiced witchcraft, and offered human sacrifices, right in the valley of Hinnom. These are possibly the worst examples of Israel's idolatry in the Bible. And it all took place in the valley of the son of Hinnom.

After Manasseh's reign and a short two-year reign of his son, Amon, Josiah, Manasseh's grandson, "did right in the sight of the Lord" and initiated reform in Judah (2 Kings 22:2). Josiah "defiled Topheth (lit., place of burning), which is in the valley of the son of Hinnom, so no man might make his son or his daughter pass through the fire of Molech" (2 Kings 23:10).

God raised up Jeremiah to support Josiah, spur on the reformation, and urge the people to repent. Jeremiah addressed the idolatry committed in the valley of the son of Hinnom, but this time Jeremiah turned the tables on the nation. Jeremiah prophesied that God would change the name of Topheth, or the valley of the son of Hinnom, to the "valley of Slaughter" and use it to discipline His unrepentant people in a future time of national chastisement (Jeremiah 7:31-32; 19:14). Thus, *Ge-hinnom* took on a future eschatological (end times) emphasis.

You can read it. It is all right there.

Gehenna is a place of future chastisement. This is exactly how Jesus spoke about it to Israel. He never spoke about this to Gentiles, who had no understanding of its historical or eschatological significance. In neither the Old Testament nor the eleven times Jesus spoke about Gehenna is it ever indicated this chastisement is eternal or unending in duration. Gehenna is not hell. For a more detailed elaboration on this subject and some expositional insights to the New Testament references, please refer to Appendix A ** (see footnotes).

For a more in-depth consideration of the references to the "second death, the lake of fire" (Revelation 2:11; 14-15; 19:20; 20:10; 21:8) and the implications of those passages, please refer to Appendix B ** (see footnotes). What we find in these verses is not what you might expect. You may come away with more questions than answers.

Damned Shame

Where does this leave us? For the purpose of this book—in order to *damn shame*—it is not necessary or feasible to deal with each particular issue in its entirety. Whole books could be, and have been, written on hell, sin, death, and wrath. A wide variety of opinions can be found on each subject. It is my hope the perspective shared here is one you will seriously weigh and consider.

Hopefully, we have at least discovered that those traditional views are not the only way to understand these passages and certainly not the best. So, in our view of God, what do we need to change to fit what we have seen? What in our thinking about God's view of us, do we need to change so we don't live in shame? How can we take this information and help others adjust their perspective of God and themselves so their own sense of worth can be strengthened and their feelings of shame can diminish and even dissolve?

- Does God see us as people who deserve damnation just for being born?
- Is the God of the Bible a God who would send the vast majority of humanity to hell for being born?
- Does the Bible clearly and explicitly reveal this severity and harshness about the character and essence of God?

The answer is: No!

There is not one verse in the Bible which clearly and explicitly says hell is the consequence of one single sin or being born in the likeness of Adam.

You read that correctly. Not one single verse in the Bible that *clearly and explicitly* says hell is the deserved consequence for being born.

Notice that each of the statements above has the phrase "clearly and explicitly" in them. This distinction is critical to the case and purpose of this chapter.

There is no denying the existence of a place that closely matches our understanding of hell: the second death, the Lake of Fire. But upon closer look at the very few verses on the Lake of Fire, we see more mystery than concrete evidence for the rigidity manifested in our theological conclusions.

The topic of hell finds more origination in Dante and the likes of non-biblical writers such as Enoch, Barruch, or Ezra (or Esdras), and in later Latin theologians than it does in the Bible. Dante writes in *Divine Comedy: Inferno* that inscribed above the door to hell is a sign that reads: *All hope abandon, ye who enter in*.[72]

The idea that it is just and right for God to punish people in His wrath for all eternity for being born with no end in sight and no redeeming value is a hard pill to swallow. It is a hope-shattering belief. If this is right, then Dante was right as well: abandon all hope.

Not only does the teaching on hell and damnation destroy hope, it opens the floodgates of shame. It distorts our view of God and how we think God views us. If people are told they deserve the worst possible fate ever imagined just for being born, is it likely they will feel they have great intrinsic value? Could there be a more destructive ideology to essential value than to think our heavenly Father considers His creatures are born like criminals deserving the worst punishment of all?

The answer is obvious.

The teaching on hell is a great contributor to shame. I recently received an email that picks up on this very problem. The email read:

> When I was fifteen and had been a Christian for three years, I was passionately trying to tell my father about Christ. I knew he would be going to hell if he died, because that's what they had told me at church. I will never forget his face and the tenor of his voice when he yelled the words, "Don't ever talk to me about this again!" You see, he couldn't and wouldn't believe in a god who would send people to hell just because they didn't have all the right beliefs.

We have all known someone who has wrestled deeply with this idea. And if they are not wrestling with it, maybe they have rejected the whole idea of God. Maybe they have blindly accepted this disagreeable teaching and tucked it away somewhere, never wanting to discuss it or admit its eerie existence. And then suddenly, someone they love dies, and they are abruptly brought face-to-face with the confrontation of this shameful belief. They are confronted with fear that their loved one who has passed is burning in the flames of hell. Fate sealed. End of story. We can't shove this topic under the bed or tuck it away on a shelf and try to live as if it's not there because death will happen. We will be faced with it again and again.

An emotional rejection of the idea won't do. Emotional reactions are not sustainable over the long haul. We need biblical reasoning. We need absolute truth from a reliable source to strengthen our sense of intrinsic worth. We need truth from God. That is why this information is so important for you, for those you love, and for those God brings across your path.

Hell has been used as a *control belief* to manipulate people to do what we think is right. Martin Luther King Jr., for example, once said, "The hottest place in hell is reserved for those who remain neutral in times of great moral conflict."[73] (King may have gotten this idea directly from Dante's *Inferno*.) King was using the scare tactic of hell to get people to join him in what he was passionate about. Sadly, the church has been doing the exact same thing for nearly 2,000 years. It is hard to imagine a more shameful or shame-causing message than to tell a human being, created in God's image, they deserve eternal damnation just because of who they are, so they better believe, do better, be better. That is so unwelcoming and uninviting. So debilitating. So condemning. So abhorrent. So untrue.

- You are not damaged.
- You are not dead.
- You are not damned.

Because you are not damaged, dead, and damned, don't live like you are. Don't hide in the bushes.

- You are capable.
- You are valuable.
- You are worthy.
- You are lovable.

Live boldly. Live confidently. Allow yourself to be loved and to love. If you choose a path of death, you will be "dead in your trespasses and sins" and you may experience His wrath for "our God is a consuming fire" (Deuteronomy 4:24; Hebrews 12:29). But God does not wish for any to perish (to waste their lives in death) but for all to come to repentance (2 Peter 3:9).

We can't live a life to the fullest apart from Jesus, for He is life. Believing in Jesus leads to life (as it was meant to be). Your odds at glory are much greater than they ever could be without Him. I think we royally mess people up with this teaching of depravity. I don't think it is having the effect those who came up with it had hoped. Let's damn the whole shameful teaching and replace it with a solid biblical perspective of humanity.

Hell is a town in Michigan; that much we can be sure. But beyond that fact, we may be left with more questions than answers. One thing is clear: we are not born DAMNED! So if we are not born damaged, dead, or damned, what is all this talk about God choosing some and not others?

---

61 Quoted from www.brainyquote.com.

62 John Piper; quoted from www.desiringgod.org: *What We Believe About the Five Points of Calvinism.*

63 R.C. Sproul, quoted from a blog on hell at Ligonier.org.

64 Ibid.

65 Dante Alighieri, *Inferno.*

66 John Milton, *Paradise Lost.*

67 Hieronymus Bosch, painter of *The Garden of Earthly Delights.*

68 Jean-Paul Sartre, quoted from www.brainyquote.com.

69 Quoted from www.goodreads.com.

70 Quoted from www.brainyquote.com.

71 See BAGD, Vines, TDNT and other lexicons/dictionaries for more information regarding this. But be warned that theological conclusions are offered in these resources which are not inherent in the words themselves.

72 Dante Alighieri, *The Divine Comedy*, Harvard Classics (1909-14).

73 Martin Luther King Jr., quoted from www.brainyquote.com.

** To view Appendix A and B, go to www.curtishtucker.com and click on "Other Offerings."

Chapter 7
Luck of the Draw

Predestination! How remote and dim.[74]
~ Dante

If there is a concept that has the potential for causing great shame, it is the belief that God chooses whom He will love and bring to heaven, and those whom He will not. Quite honestly, the whole idea of such a doctrine is gross and detestable to me. In fact, an in-depth study and research on this particular subject more than ten years ago is what led to many freedoms since that time in my own understanding and walk with the Lord. It was through this window that a whole new way of thinking blew in and breathed fresh perspective and life.

Now the idea seems even more grotesque and destructive than it did before.

Think back to Mike from chapter one, the young boy whose heart was crushed by the abrasive and powerful words of his father. In Mike's child mind and understanding, he was being rejected. He was not good enough. He was not chosen by his father for love, affirmation, or worth. The pain of that is a hard pill to swallow, and the shame that ensues is understandable.

It's one thing for that to happen to a child from his father, but it's even more devastating to be told, and believe it to be true, that your Creator—who wove you together in your mother's womb and placed every atom, molecule, and DNA together to make you who you are—doesn't want you.

If we live in a world created by God and for God, and we are created by Him and for Him, but this God is selective in His goodness and grace for any reason whatsoever, then all is not right with the world. It is a society in which kids are to be seen but not heard, where undesirables go hungry and in need, and those who can't stick up for themselves are waiting and longing to see if the roulette wheel of goodness and grace will fall on their number. It is a world too big, or too bad, to deserve grace, so only those who hit the divine lottery find reason to rejoice. But who can know, I mean really know for sure, that his number will be called? What does he do until he knows? How can he survive not knowing if he is chosen? What if he believes he will never be chosen or that he is not worthy to be selected?

I honestly search for positives in this line of thinking, but always—I mean *always*—come up empty. The idea that only a select group is chosen is devastating. The idea that a "God of love" does not love all the same is seriously troubling. But that's exactly what the teaching of predestination and unconditional election tells us. It essentially says God doesn't love everyone. He only loves those He picks and chooses to bring to heaven while all the rest get what they deserve and must rot in hell for all eternity.

But it is worse yet. Election is, as we have been taught, the notion that God picks who will believe and consequently spend eternity with Him in heaven, and who will not believe and, therefore, spend eternity in hell separated from Him. According to the *experts*, God determines who will actually believe and who will not believe. This is due to the idea that man, in a fallen state, is incapable of believing, and God must sovereignly choose whom to grace with faith. If God has chosen, then those who are chosen cannot *not* believe. God's choice determines faith.

I recently listened to a recorded sermon by a popular pastor, having this persuasion on the doctrine of election. In the message he gave on this topic, he referred to this sacred teaching as "Duck, Duck, Damned."[75] This is an obvious play off the old children's game Duck, Duck, Goose. This is exactly what he, or anyone who holds to this teaching, is saying when they teach election: God chooses who will believe and go to heaven. On the other hand, He chooses who will not believe and will spend eternity in hell ... *Duck, Duck, DAMNED!*

Not a humorous analogy by any stretch. This idea of election is not true; it is a fabrication. And it is divisive and destructive.

Unconditional election is a hazardous teaching and an enemy to the cross of Christ. God offers love and acceptance at His own cost to the whole world. To say otherwise is to say the cross was insufficient.

To say otherwise makes God's love conditional and only to some, to those whom He chooses. This is exactly what Satan would love for us to think because it causes shame and hiding. It causes us to never be fully sure of where we stand with God. It causes us to question our worth and lovability. It causes us to question and doubt the integrity and nature of God Himself. All that needs to happen for us to move from security to shame is a bit of doubt or fear. Even a tiny bit of uncertainty about who God is can cause us to feel shame and want to hide—and for truth to have less weight in the scale. It causes us to hide in the bushes because we fear disconnection. This uncertainty springs from doubt and fear.

Quite frankly, I don't get the logic of such a teaching.

In this system of theology—this house of cards—God actually gives faith to those whom He has chosen *so that* they will believe. This is very disturbing. Apparently, God holds all people accountable on the condition of faith in His Son. Yet, it is God Himself who chooses and then gives the faith, thereby determining that they will believe while others—who have not been chosen nor given the faith—could not believe. Do you see the discrepancies here?

According to this teaching, once the pick was made (in eternity past), the fate of all who would ever live was sealed. The theological tradition suggests, and wants you to think, this doctrine answers the question: *Why is anyone saved?* The answer: *Because God chose them.* Notice the past tense nature of their answer.

This teaching actually surfaced fairly late in church history, even though it seems rather old looking back on it now. This teaching came to acceptance through much debate over God's sovereignty and man's free will in the latter part of the fourth century into the early part of the fifth century, most notably in the debates between St. Augustine of Hippo and a British theologian living in Rome named Pelagius. The debate dealt with the issue of how a man could be saved and how grace operates in salvation.

Augustine believed that on account of the Fall, in Adam, man is so totally depraved that his affections are completely and utterly evil. Thus, for man to get saved, God must change his affections first, which He does for those He chooses. This was not the view of the church fathers that preceded Augustine, such as St. Irenaeus, Tertullian, Clement of Alexandria, and Origen, and it is not the view of many in the Eastern Church today.

Even in St. Augustine's day, there was much opposition to his new view, yet the Augustinian tradition eventually won out and marks a significant shift in Western thought and theology that is alive and thriving to this day. But even long-standing traditions can have a cloak of darkness. Clark H. Pinnock wrote about this darkness and from where it came:

> Dark thoughts have clouded our minds. For centuries, thanks largely to the Augustinian tradition that has so influenced evangelicals, we have been taught that God chooses a few who will be saved and has not decided to save a vast majority of humanity.[76]

A dark thought indeed.

This Augustinian doctrine of predestination was denied at the Council of Orange (A.D. 529), only to be revived later in the Reformation. It became more doggedly solidified in such reformers as Luther and Calvin and their successors. As a result, predestination and election have become basic assumptions in traditional Christian teaching, accepted by most, and yet hated by many (even by some who accept it). Why is it so dark? What could devastate and destroy our sense of worth and sense of belonging more than the idea that our heavenly Father and Creator may or may not have chosen us? That His love is a matter of *will* or *will not*.

Not long ago, I met with a husband and wife about a ceremony they were to participate in with their child. I knew the father did not come to church and had some reservations about what he called "organized religion." The ceremony was going to direct some questions at each of them, so I wanted to get a better handle on where he was spiritually. As the conversation progressed, he stated, "I cannot believe in a God who picks some for heaven and others He condemns to hell." Now we were getting to the heart of the matter.

This is an all too common objection because many people have a hard time with the conflicting views of God. As we continued to talk about this and other related subjects, I could see the pain, anger, and shame from years of spiritual abuse. It all came flooding out that day as if it had been pent up for years. We went ahead with the ceremony, but with his permission I shared openly about where he was with his belief in God. The ceremony was extremely moving for all in attendance. I wish I could say he had a lightning bolt conversion experience, but I do know it was an important step in his ongoing journey to return to the God of his youth. Sometimes, just taking a brick off the wall that hinders people from walking with God is all we can hope for.

Many people object to the idea of Duck, Duck, Damned, or election and predestination, but without adequate understanding and explanations of the passages in the Bible that have been traditionally used to impose this teaching, these people either shelve the issue, avoid those passages, or they choose a church/religion where it is not an issue. Trying to reconcile this idea that God picks and chooses who gets to go to heaven and who will go to hell with the fact that God has clearly revealed Himself as a God who is love, has troubled many and caused some to quit trying to make sense of it—or just quit altogether.

Unconditional election is a theological idea built on complex systems of man's reason. It is not based on God's thoughts or His ways.

Our thoughts, especially in this case, are not His thoughts.

We ought not sit out, shelve the issue, nor use the "His thoughts are not our thoughts" excuse to blindly accept what we cannot reconcile. We have foisted our thoughts upon God because we have not rightly understood His thoughts.

And the offshoots of this distorted view of God are equally destructive.

Unholy Appendages

The teaching of election is not without many destructive tentacles.

Some who reject—even if purely on an emotional basis—the ideas of election and predestination, unknowingly or ignorantly hold to the tenets of this teaching by clinging to one or more of these by-products of election.

One unholy appendage of predestination and election is the corresponding doctrine of perseverance of the saints, which for St. Augustine was itself a gift along with faith.

At the core of the demand that all saints persevere in a life of good works as evidence that they are saved (i.e., one of God's chosen) is a performance-based means of acceptance. This is conditional acceptance, and it is a strong, albeit subtle at times, reinforcer of shame. This is the idea that *if* you really are a Christian, it will show. But *if* it does not show, you have no reason to believe you are a Christian.

If we are talking about someone else we say things like: "She says she is a Christian, but by the way she is living, she must not be." If it doesn't show, to whatever degree someone sets the standards, then you likely were never saved to begin with. In accordance with the doctrines of election and predestination, this simply means you must not have been chosen in the first place. Thus, you must always persevere in order to prove (to *whom* I have no idea) you are what you think and say you are. This is not graceful living; this is disgraceful.

This is crazy talk. Your walk with God will become evident, but your standing, worth, and acceptance before God is not tied to what you do, but who you are—and most importantly, who God is. God offers acceptance at His own cost: the cross of His only Son.

Another common outworking of this teaching is spiritual elitism: the pride and arrogance that comes from thinking we are superior to others. Prideful thinking leads very naturally to being judgmental and condemnatory. Shame researcher Brené Brown writes:

> Finding someone to put down, judge, or criticize becomes a way to get out of the web or call attention away from our own box. If you're doing worse than I am at something, I think my chances of surviving are better … we're constantly serving up the people around us as more deserving prey … what is ironic … we judge people in areas where we're vulnerable to shame.[77]

If that is not a Polaroid snapshot of the church, I don't know what is. And this picture differs very little from that of first century Judaism, especially evident in the Pharisees who interacted with Jesus. Israel's arrogance stemmed from thinking they alone were God's *only* choice.[78] They shrouded over their judgmentalism with religious verbiage, much the same way we do today.

Rigidly hypercritical and condemnatory people find it easier and more pleasant to focus on someone else's sin instead of their own. Who is going to throw the first stone? The tentacles of predestination and election are far-reaching. There are numerous beliefs held by Christians today that find their roots in this teaching, but most of us don't understand that. We hold on to these ideas because we've always heard them. We've always believed them, and people we esteem have always held them too. But as we delve into the teaching of election and predestination, my hope is that you will be able to see the house of cards for what it is, and how the beliefs many of us hold will be buried under that house as it collapses.

The teaching of election and predestination (and its offshoots) leads us to live a life of discouragement and defeat, deceived into thinking we must perform and be perfect—at least better than the guy next to us—in order to be accepted. The teaching undermines our confident assurance of our standing and worth with God, and it undermines the nature and character of God Himself. Like Mike, we hear the voice of a father in our hearts telling us we aren't worthy of love, we aren't worthy to be chosen, or that others aren't worthy of His love.

This perception of God and His view of us will lead to a life of running away from God, sitting life out, or tirelessly striving to please people and God just to stay in good graces. When we make performance the condition for assurance, the path is anything but reassuring or restful. One could hardly say their yoke is easy or their burden light (Matthew 11:30).

Relationships are supposed to be safe and secure. We want to feel loved and that we belong. Relationships driven by people trying to control and manipulate by keeping us guessing are not good, healthy relationships. Our intrinsic significance and worth in God's eyes are not related to our performance. We see ourselves judged that way because our view of God is wrong.

Clark H. Pinnock wrote that election "manages to make bad news out of good news. It casts a deep shadow over the character of God."[79]

Bad news out of good news? A deep shadow over the character of God? A simple reading of Genesis will help a person see and understand that from the beginning, God does make some choices, but His choosing has nothing whatsoever to do with who is going to heaven and who is going to hell. Election has nothing to do with eternal salvation as we understand it.

God's election has nothing to do with the eternal fate of human beings. Choosing some and not others is not about eternal destinies. God's choosing (i.e., His election) has a temporal purpose, a purpose for time with a beginning and ending. God's choice of one person or tribe over another was about temporal promises He was giving to those individuals or groups that would be fulfilled on this earth, within time. God's choice is about selecting a servant to use and bring about blessings for the whole world through His chosen vessel. Election is not about eternity and certainly not about the eternal destinies of individuals, corporately or individually.

Election is not about eternal salvation at all. Election is not about who God chooses to believe so that those who believe will go to heaven when they die. Election is not about God predetermining who will not believe and, therefore, go to everlasting torment when they die. If election is not about eternal destiny in heaven, then non-election (usually referred to as *the passing over* of individuals and leaving them on their own) is not about eternal destiny in hell.

More plainly stated, if being "chosen" isn't about being chosen to go to heaven, then not being chosen isn't about being damned to hell for all eternity. The God created in the doctrine of unconditional election is not the God revealed in the Bible, and once you see the truth of who He is, you will breathe a sigh of relief.

---

74 Quoted from www.thinkexist.com.

75 Mark Driscoll, recording at www.marshill.com/2008/01/21/predestination-duck-duck-damned.

76 Clark H. Pinnock, *A Wideness in God's Mercy*, pp.19, 25.

77 Brené Brown, *Daring Greatly*, p98, 99.

78 We will see in later chapters that God's choice of Israel was that they would be a means through which God would bring light and reconciliation to the whole world. This obviously indicates that they, Israel, were not God's only choice.

79 Clark H. Pinnock, *A Wideness in God's Mercy*, p.2.

Chapter 8
Down the Rabbit Hole

The beginning is the most important part of the work.[80]
~ Plato

Alice: Would you tell me, please, which way I ought to go from here?
The Cheshire Cat: That depends a good deal on where you want to get to.
Alice: I don't much care where.
The Cheshire Cat: Then it doesn't much matter which way you go.
Alice: So long as I get somewhere.
The Cheshire Cat: Oh, you're sure to do that, if only you walk long enough.

~ Lewis Carroll, Alice's Adventures in Wonderland[81]

I hope it is safe to say we share a desired destination of a better understanding of who God is and to clear up any confusion we may have about Him. It is undeniable that an idea of "choosing" exists in the Bible, so it says something about God. But not what most people think. We have to get to that understanding, and that is precisely where we are going.

We are going somewhere important.

Where we end up is directly tied to how we start our journey. If we don't care much about where we end—as Alice didn't care in *Alice's Adventures in Wonderland*—then wandering lost in the woods is a likely scenario for us. You may be there right now. Lost. Wandering (or possibly wondering). Searching for a destination you aren't sure of, but certain you haven't arrived.

To start the journey, we need to start at the beginning—where else?—and stick close to the stepping-stones in Scripture so we don't wander off the path.

Just as Alice discovered, there are plenty of rabbit trails to follow and holes to fall into. We must be good path-walkers and watch our step as we allow His Word to be a lamp to our feet and light to our path (Psalm 119:105). As the psalmist sang, "The unfolding of Your words gives light; it gives understanding to the simple" (Psalm 119:130).

What is the truth behind the fact that God's Word tells us some are *chosen*? What was God's intention for election from the beginning?

Down the rabbit hole.

I hope you are as surprised and amazed as I was when I first saw how simple this whole thing is, and how easy it is to clear up any confusion as we find our way to our destination.

But first, let me set the scene so you know why election is even a topic of discussion.

From the Whole to Some

In the beginning, God planted a garden and placed man and woman there, telling them to be fruitful, multiply, and rule and subdue the earth (Genesis 1:26, 28; 2:8, 15). This was God's kingdom objective given to man. Man was in the Garden having unbroken fellowship with God. He had a purpose and a plan, and it was "very good" (Genesis 1:31). The serpent, however, lied to mankind by deceptively convincing the man and woman God was holding out on them. Adam and Eve bought the lie and ate the fruit.

Mankind failed. Strike one.

God gave out curses (or consequences) to all parties involved (see Genesis 3:14-19). After covering the nakedness of the man and woman (Genesis 3:21), God cast them out, east of the Garden, to work the ground (Genesis 3:23-24). Mankind was out of the Garden—the land God had made for them—but man still had a relationship with God. God went with them eastward. Just read the story. God stayed with them. They did not have to do anything, say anything, walk an aisle, or commit to anything. While they lost *fellowship* with God momentarily, they never lost their *relationship* with God, and God was still committed to them. They did not have to be saved from hell. They did not need to be chosen to go to heaven. God had relationship with Adam, Eve, Abel, and even Cain. God was working with humanity as one group.

After the death of Abel, Cain was banished farther eastward, and God provided an offspring to Adam and Eve in the place of Abel: Seth. And "men began to call upon the name of the Lord" (Genesis 4:26). God was the God of all. There was no division of loved and unloved, saved and unsaved. And we know for certain that men walked with God, and God walked with them (Genesis 5:22, 24).

As time went on, man multiplied on the face of the earth, but so did wickedness, even to the point that their thoughts were wicked all the time (Genesis 6:8).

Mankind failed ... again.

Strike two.

It grieved God and made Him sorry He ever made man, so He blotted every living being off the face of the earth by flood, except the eight God chose to deliver and serve Him. The reason God chose Noah and his family was not because they were the only people on the planet who knew God or that God loved, but because they were the only ones who were apparently trusting God. They were blameless and upright in the way they lived.

Noah and his family walked with God (Genesis 6:9).

Their deliverance from death (by escaping the flood) was because they were walking with God. Those who died in the flood experienced God's chastisement for acting wickedly and were banished from the earth. That is all we know, but it is all we need to know. What we can be sure of is this: those whom God loves, He disciplines and even scourges (Hebrews 12:6).

Mankind had failed, but God had a plan to "reboot," so to speak.

Noah and his family were chosen to remain and carry forth the prospect and promise of God's kingdom upon this earth. They would represent all of mankind going forward. God was still committed to working with humanity, now the descendants of Noah, as a whole.

After their long, stormy boat ride, the earth dried up, and Noah and his family got off the ark and started all over again. God said "in his heart" that He would never again destroy every living thing by water (Genesis 8:21). God made an everlasting covenant with Noah and his sons. The covenant was a promise never to destroy the earth by water, and the sign was the rainbow (Genesis 9:8-17).

Have you seen any rainbows lately? As a reminder of God's gracious covenant with all humanity, it is better than a pot of gold.

What is important to notice is that God reiterated the blessing of creation—to be fruitful, multiply, and have dominion (Genesis 1:26-28)—upon Noah and his sons (Genesis 8:17; 9:1, 19). He told them to disseminate over the whole earth.[82] This was God's way of empowering them to fulfill their function as vice-regents over the whole earth—an important directive that they would soon fail to follow when they gathered together in Babel. More on that later.

Unfortunately, there was another sinful moment that threw a bit of a wrinkle in what otherwise was a perfect plan. Noah partook in a little too much of the fruit of his vine and acted foolishly (Genesis 9:21). Ham saw the nakedness of his father and told his brothers with delight (Genesis 9:22). Shem and Japheth did not find this a laughing matter and covered their father (Genesis 9:23).

But the damage was done.

As a result of this, Noah cursed Canaan, the son of Ham. And in cursing Canaan, God was also putting Shem and Japheth in a priority position of service and blessing, yet only one of these two would be in the ultimate choice position. What is clear from the blessing and cursing is that the one son who is given a priority place of service is Shem, for even Japheth is going to dwell in the tents of Shem (Genesis 9:26-27).

Shem was the chosen line of service and blessing. Shem was the elect. The blessings promised were temporal blessings, not eternal. Equally, the curse is not an eternal curse to hell. Shem is not singled out as the only one who is going to get to go to heaven when he dies.

And for the most part, things went along fine ... for a while. Sadly, man failed yet again.

Mankind did not fill the earth, but gathered in one place trying to make a name for themselves. They built a tower to heaven, trying to take God's place (Genesis 11:1-9).

Man failed again. Strike three.

God had graciously worked with humankind as one lump sum even despite sin, but now it would be different. In fact, it would never be the same, at least not exactly.

As a consequence to their sinful, collective efforts at Babel, God confused their language and scattered them abroad over the face of the whole earth (Genesis 11:9).

He spread them out Himself, but He did not banish them from the face of the earth. Three times God had worked with all humanity: at creation, after the Fall, and after the flood. Three times He graciously began, but three times mankind failed.

The result was that they were *SCATTERED*.

Yet God was not fatally frustrated in His plans for this earth or for humanity. He was, however, going to take a new tactic. This is the place where things changed, and the place where the concept of being chosen becomes clearly evident. Because people were spread out over the face of the earth, God began to draw out a specific people for His own possession for special service in order to use them to reach the whole world for His kingdom purpose. God loves all and has chosen all humanity to serve Him and fulfill their created purpose, but was now, in light of their rebellion, choosing a select group to gather the affections and service of all. Ingenious. Now the chosen idea is going to pick up steam.

Chosen:

- **Shem**—not Japheth, and not Canaan.
- **Arpachshad**—not Elam, not Asshur, not Lud, nor Aram.
- **Shelah**
- **Eber**
- **Peleg**—not Joktan
- **Serug**, **Nahor**, **Terah** … and then,
- Of the sons of Terah, not Nahor, not Haran … but **Abram**.

This is the shortened version. You can read the details in Genesis 10:21-11:32.

This, in a nutshell, is the progression of God's choice: election. This is election to special service for God and His purposes.

When we look at the lineage from Noah all the way to Abram, we see that names are highlighted in Scripture. We see Shem, Arpachsad, Shelah, to Peleg and Rue, to Abram. This is the lineage of the ones God chose for His one, particular, temporal purpose: the purpose of bringing the heel to crush the serpent for the establishment of His kingdom on this earth through the seed of the woman, and ultimately Messiah.

The focus of God's election is going to turn sharply in a positive way to the person and life of Abram and his relationship with God, later called the God of Abraham, and the blessings that are promised to him and his seed.

Take a look. God called Abram to an undisclosed country, and he went (Genesis 12:1-4). And here is what God promised (Genesis 12:2-3):

- "I will make you a great nation."
- "I will bless you."
- "You shall be a blessing, and I will bless those who bless you."
- "The one who curses you I will curse."
- "In you all the families of the earth shall be blessed."

But the heart of the promise entails a certain piece of real estate: "To your descendants I will give this land" (Genesis 12:7).

Later, God would confirm this promise of the land by ratifying a covenant with Abram (Genesis 15:17-18). This is a guaranteed covenant even though it has conditions to be met in order for the fulfillment to take place. What is guaranteed? God will have a people of His own possession who are of the descendants of Abram. They will possess the Promised Land, serve God, and be a source of blessing to the whole world.

Abram is chosen to be the representative of God to the whole world. He is chosen to be the source of blessing for the whole world.

God's selection of Abram for this unique purpose is the commencement of election, and it had to do with God's temporal plan and purposes. In no way, as we will see, is election about who gets to go to heaven when they die. Election is about the temporal plan of God to establish His kingdom upon this earth through a people of His own possession, a people who will be a kingdom of priests to God so that all the nations of the earth may be blessed.

This is about temporal blessings, temporal promises, and a temporal covenant—not eternal. The exclusion of other descendants from the focus or the specific blessings that will be promised to Abram does not mean God was not also, in a broader sense, the God of the whole world, of all people. Because God chose a specific line to serve Him—through which He would bring about the specific promises of restoration of all things—did not mean He did not love others or have a relationship with them, or choose them for other purposes or service.

God wants to bless all people.

The silence on the other descendants of Peleg or Joktan, or any other line of Shem or even his brother Japheth—and yes, even the descendants of Ham, including Canaan—does not mean they are "unbelievers" doomed to hell for all eternity, nor that their position is one of shame. Those who are not chosen to fulfill a similar purpose to that of Israel's are not less valuable or less lovable. And while they may have experienced some disappointment if they had even known what God was doing—which I doubt they did at the time—it is not as if they were discarded by God or unloved. They simply were not chosen for this particular line of service for God to bring about blessings for the whole earth. They will all ultimately share in the blessings of God's kingdom when it is established on this earth, but they are not the vessels through which the Messiah will initially come.

Satan wants us to believe God chooses some, eternally speaking, for good and others for evil ... that He loves some and despises the rest, some for heaven, the rest for hell. But that isn't what Scripture tells us.

This story is about what God is doing on earth, within time. This story is about the temporal blessings flowing from a personal Messiah and which line they would come through after the separation of humankind at the tower of Babel. This is the *salvation* God has planned for the creation and His creatures. This is why God chose Abram.

As Clark Pinnock recognizes:

> The decision to call Abram designates the path God has chosen to bring about the salvation of the many through faith of the one, the principle of representation ... The election of Abram is evidence of God's desire to save the world.[83]

The salvation to which God had chosen Abram will take place in time and upon this earth in the land that God has promised. Making promises to Abram and his descendants was God's way of "choosing some on behalf of many."[84]

Further Down the Rabbit Hole

This same purpose of choosing continues. Watch the connection to the New Testament. Quite honestly, this is where the light bulb started to come on for me in the pursuit of understanding the nature and purpose of God's choosing.

The Genesis story continues and focuses in on the descendants of Abram. If we skip ahead in the story, it says Isaac was chosen, not Ishmael (the firstborn to Abram). Jacob, not Esau (the firstborn to Isaac).

The point is to teach that blessings bestowed are not a *right*. They are an act of *grace*. These are important links in the chain because:

> For they are not all Israel who are descended from Israel; nor are they all children because they are Abraham's descendants, but THROUGH ISAAC YOUR DESCENDANTS WILL BE NAMED (Romans 9:6-7).

And:

> Just as it is written, "JACOB I LOVED, BUT ESAU I HATED" (Romans 9:13).

The apostle Paul considered these important facts in writing to the church at Rome, so they must be important to us as well. Miss the links of this chain and the nature or purpose of God's choice here, and you will have no foundation for understanding passages like this, among others that discuss the topic of election in the New Testament. And if you have nothing to go on, you will be left, as many have been, to invent a new idea for election that is not based in the Bible. So many people want to make these passages in the New Testament about God choosing who is going to heaven and who is going to hell, but that is totally inconsistent with the historical nature of these passages in the Old Testament.

What in Genesis do we see revealed as to the nature and purpose of God's choices of one over another? God chose Abram and revealed to him exactly why He had chosen him: to bless him, to make him a great nation, to give him a land, to bless all the families of the earth through him, and to bring a king forth through his descendants.

God unfolded these promises to Abram, and Abram took them and ran with them. Abram understood that if he was going to be a father of a great nation, he first had to have a child. Makes sense, right?

The apparent hindrance in this plan was the barrenness of his wife Sarai. So off Abram ran, with the help of his wife, to *assist* God in the fulfillment of His promise. Abram had sexual relations with his wife's Egyptian maid, Hagar, and she bore him a son. He had a son of his own agenda; he was running the show. But as Paul would later write: "So then it does not depend upon the man who wills or the man who runs, but on God who has mercy" (Romans 9:16).

Abram ran, but God had a different plan.

God Hears and Laughs

Things didn't go exactly as Abram and Sarai imagined, especially for Sarai. She became jealous of Hagar (and Hagar actually despised Sarai for not having children). But Sarai had more pull in the house and treated Hagar harshly. So Hagar left town (Genesis 16:6).

But watch this. It is not what you might expect.

The text says, "Now the angel of the Lord found her" (Hagar, Genesis 16:7) and told her to return to Sarai (Genesis 16:9). Then he blessed her and said, "I will greatly multiply your descendants so that they will be too many to count" (Genesis 16:10).

Did you catch that? This is a nice little side plot.

God blesses Hagar and says her descendants through her son will be blessed. This sounds a lot like the original blessing God gave to Adam, Eve (Genesis 1:28), and Noah (Genesis 8:17, 9:1).

God told her to name her son Ishmael, which means "God hears," because God was compassionate to her affliction. Despite the goodness of God and blessings upon Ishmael, this one was not going to be the son through which the promises God gave to Abram would come.

It does not depend on man who runs, but on God who has mercy.

Despite the futility of Abram's own plan, God remains faithful to His plan and promise and appears again (Genesis 17:1). This time, God changes Abram's name to Abraham, which means "father of many." He reaffirms the promise that Abraham will be a father of nations and kings, the covenant is everlasting, and the land will be the possession of his descendants. God gave him a sign, circumcision, to observe in accordance with the covenant. Then God tells Abraham that Sarai is getting a new name—Sarah—and will be having a bun in the oven, even at her ripe old age of ninety. God even goes so far as to give Abraham the name of his son: Isaac, which means "he laughs." Sarah laughed, but God has the last laugh on this one.

It is through Sarah, not Hagar, the promise would come.

It is through Isaac, not Ishmael, the blessings are passed.

The child Sarah will bear to Abraham will be a son, and his name shall be called Isaac. It is Isaac through whom God says the covenant will be guaranteed, not Ishmael. Ishmael will be blessed, but not with the blessings of God's covenant which He made with Abraham (Genesis 17:20-21). That would only be through Isaac. God made a choice.

This is precisely Paul's point when he reminds the Roman believers that not all physical descendants of Abraham are children of promise, but "through Isaac your descendants will be named" (Romans 9:7-8). Romans 9 will be discussed at length later, but for now it should be clear that the historical choosing of Isaac over Ishmael was not about who was going to heaven and who was going to hell, but about who was going to serve God and get the promises of the covenant God made with Abraham. Election in Genesis had a temporal purpose. The election in Genesis is the same being discussed by Paul in Romans 9. Election is about what God has planned for the whole earth, brought about through specific people who will serve Him and possess a specific land—the Promised Land—which will be the center of His kingdom.

The links of the chain continue.

Flip-Flopped

The next thing we see in the ongoing development of the election purposes of God is in twin sons born to Isaac and his wife, Rebekah.

This is the place where we see a divine flip-flop, a reversal of the natural order.

The pregnancy was not an easy one for Rebekah for the "children struggled together within her" (Genesis 25:22), so she sought wisdom and understanding from the Lord. The Lord answered her inquiry by enlightening her to His elective purpose: "Two nations are in your womb; and two peoples shall be separated from your body; and one people shall be stronger than the other; and the older shall serve the younger" (Genesis 25:23). That is a total flip-flop from how things normally were done. The firstborn, the older, usually received a greater portion and responsibility. But God chose the younger, Jacob, over the older, Esau.

For *what* did God choose Jacob over Esau? And *why* did God choose Jacob over Esau?

First of all, God did not choose because of anything inherently good or evil in either of them. Neither did God choose because of anything they did in the womb, or ever would do out of it. It was simply God's choice. In the words of Paul, "... for though the twins were not yet born and had not done anything good or bad, so that God's purpose according to His choice would stand, not because of works, but because of Him who calls, it was said to her, 'THE OLDER SHALL SERVE THE YOUNGER'" (Romans 9:11-12). God had made a choice, albeit contrary to the natural order of how things typically would go. The older shall *serve* the younger to show His power and purposes to fulfill the covenant He Himself had guaranteed to Abraham and Isaac.

So for what did God choose?

God chose Jacob to be the one who would uniquely serve Him and the one to whom He would show His covenant loyalty. The older shall serve the younger, so the younger was going to be preeminent. It is for this very reason that Paul, quoting the prophet Malachi, could write: "Just as it is written, 'JACOB I LOVED, BUT ESAU I HATED'" (Romans 9:13). This is the place where we generally get all theologically clever and wander off the biblical reservation. But we must be careful not to rush to conclusions here. The love God showed unto Jacob was His covenant love, a love called *chesed* in the Old Testament. The hate God had for Esau was not like we think of hate. It was simply an indifference to Esau as it related to the blessings and promises of the covenant that would be given to those who served. Certainly, a God of love also loved Esau with an eternal love and greatly blessed Esau (see Genesis 33). This much is safe to assume, but what is clear is that God lovingly and mercifully made a choice between two twins, neither of which deserved or merited God's covenant, in order to show His power and sovereignty over the matter of His blessings.

But remember, we are talking about temporal promises and blessings, not spiritualized, eternal blessings. This is not, nor was it ever, about who is going to get to go to heaven when they die and who is going to some other place we call hell.

Esau did bear a grudge against Jacob (Genesis 27:41) because Jacob received their father's blessing, but apparently that hatchet was buried, and Esau warmly received Jacob back from Padam-Aram. Later, Esau left the land of promise and settled in the land of Seir, which is a historical outworking of God's choosing Jacob for the promise and blessing. God loves those who live in Seir as well. It is just that Seir is not the land God intends to bless, and Esau's descendants are not the direct line of people through which God wills to bring the blessings.

Jacob He loved, but Esau He hated.

Let's explore this love and hate thing a bit more. An illustration may be helpful. And we have a wonderful illustration right in the book of Genesis.

Jacob had two wives but not by his own choosing. The wife he loved was Rachel (Genesis 29:18). His other wife, Leah, the older sister of Rachel, was the wife that Laban tricked Jacob into marrying because she was his oldest daughter. We read in the story that "the Lord saw that Leah was unloved" by Jacob (Genesis 29:31). The word translated as "unloved," interestingly enough, is the Hebrew word *sane* which means *to hate, turn against*. It bears the idea here that Leah is the one "not chosen" and to whom Jacobs's affections did not fall on in the same way as they did Rachel.

I am sure Jacob treated Leah well. He shared a life with her, but she was unloved because she was not his first choice. So as it related to the covenant of marriage, Jacob loved Leah less because he loved Rachel more.

This theme of *love* and *hate* will be a theme God brings back later in the prophets and most memorably in the writing of the apostle Paul (Malachi 1:2; Romans 9:13). Hate does not mean what you thought. Hate means to love less or to be indifferent towards someone as it relates to blessings.

This is the same idea behind the words of Jesus when He told the disciples, "If anyone comes to Me, and does not hate his own father and mother and wife and children and brothers and sisters, yes, and even his own life, he cannot be My disciple" (Luke 14:26).

A parallel passage states it oppositely when Jesus said, "He who loves father or mother *more than* Me is not worthy of Me; and he who loves son or daughter *more than* Me is not worthy of Me" (Matthew 10:37).

The point is uniqueness by comparison, not exclusivity. When it comes to being a disciple of Jesus, we must differentiate between two very different kinds of love: the one we have for our family and the one we have for the Lord Jesus. Both are real love, but they are different manifestations. This difference in love may cause us to be indifferent to others in our life in comparison to what He is asking of us.

Back to Jacob and Esau.

God loved both Jacob and Esau, but as it related to the blessings He wanted to bestow, He made a choice to love Jacob in one way and Esau in another.

Onward with the links in the chain.

Jacob becomes a focus of Genesis—and the entire Bible for that matter—because he has twelve sons combined from his two wives and their handmaids. These sons comprised the twelve tribes of Israel (Genesis 29:31-35; 29:1-24; 35:18).

While much of the narrative in Genesis is devoted to the life of Joseph, the purpose behind the events of his life is for a *greater* purpose: "to preserve life … a remnant in the earth … to preserve many people alive" (Genesis 45:5, 7; 50:20) for the nation of Israel.

Even within the twelve sons of Israel, all are chosen to serve God, but the service of one of the sons is unique. Of the twelve sons, the chosen one through whom the Messianic blessing would come was his fourth-born son, Judah. The reason, according to Genesis, is because Reuben, Jacob's firstborn son, disqualified himself because he liked to sleep in his daddy's bed when his dad was away—but his concubine was not (Genesis 35:22; 49:3-4). The blessing would also skip over the second and third-born sons, Simeon and Levi. Both are apparently skipped over because of their anger as it was expressed when they went on their vengeful killing spree on Hamor and Shechem and the men of their city (Genesis 34:25-30; 50:5-7).

So, the King to come, and thus the kingdom, would come through Judah. This is evident in the blessing of Jacob on Judah: "The scepter shall not depart from Judah, nor the ruler's staff from between his feet, until Shiloh {*the one to whom it belongs*} comes, and to him shall be the obedience of the peoples" (Genesis 49:10). The prophetic hope of Messiah would usher in a new age of great abundance as well: "He ties his foal to the vine, and his donkey's colt to the choice vine; He washes his garments in wine, and his robes in the blood of grapes. His eyes are dull from wine, and his teeth white from milk" (Genesis 49:11-12). That is a poetic way of saying it will be a time of great celebration, a time of great abundance, and a time of great obedience.

These are very important blessings given to Judah, but all the twelve tribes of Israel are blessed when "he [Jacob] blessed them. He blessed them, every one with the blessing appropriate to him" (Genesis 49:28). The whole nation of Israel, the twelve tribes, will be a blessed nation. What is apparent is that from this time forward, God is the God of Israel.

But don't jump to the wrong conclusion as so many seem to do. Just because God is the God of Israel—as it relates to His plan to bring about the blessings and promises given to Abraham—He is still a God who loves the whole world.

He has chosen Israel for a purpose: to be *light to the whole world*. But first, the nation had to spend four hundred years in Egypt as God had told Abram many years prior (Genesis 15:13).

While the final years in Egypt were anything but the best years for the nation of Israel, God heard their cry and "remembered His covenant with Abraham, Isaac, and Jacob" (Exodus 2:24). Hopefully, we remember what the covenant was about that God was then remembering. Land. Blessing. All nations.

For God to *remember* the covenant, He had to get Israel out of Egypt and into the land He had promised to Abraham. To deliver the nation, God would send Moses.

Possessive God

To deliver the nation, God sent Moses to display His power to Pharaoh so that he might "know that there is no one like Me in all the earth … in order to show you My power and in order to proclaim My name through all the earth" (Exodus 9:13, 16). When Moses encounters God in the burning bush, God reveals Himself to Moses as "the God of your father, the God of Abraham, the God of Isaac, and the God of Jacob" (Exodus 3:6). Later, when Moses asked God for an additional moniker just in case the sons of Israel might ask, God responded with His personal name, Yahweh (Exodus 3:14). God also refers to Himself as "the God of the Hebrews" (Exodus 4:18) and calls Israel "My son, My first-born" (Exodus 4:22).

None of these particular and covenantal monikers, for God Himself or Israel, intend to imply that God is not also the God of the Egyptians, the Canaanites, and the whole world for that matter. God remains a God of all people and has a covenant with all the descendants of Noah.

He has a plan for Egypt and all mankind even though He will now accomplish His global purposes through the chosen nation of Israel. For God to accomplish His purpose, He had to ransom Israel from the land of Egypt, from the hand of Pharaoh, and bring them back in to the land and give them rest. He delivered them so that the nation could "serve" God (Exodus 8:1, 20; 9:13) … not be the only people who go to heaven. This is an honorable use (Romans 9:21) while Pharaoh would be used for common purposes (Romans 9:17).

In order for the rest to be realized, the nation had to be faithful to Yahweh and to His purposes for them. They were anything but.

The remainder of the Old Testament is a history of the tumultuous relationship of God with Israel and their rebellion against Him. But God, in His grace and mercy, remained faithful and promised a New Covenant in the future, even if it will only come after much tribulation.

When Jesus began His ministry, it was the same message: "Repent, for the kingdom of heaven is at hand" (Matthew 4:17).

Jesus was remembering the covenant with Abraham, Isaac, and Jacob.

Follow the White Rabbit

Christians have spent hundreds of years down the rabbit hole of misunderstanding Scripture, floundering in a pool of tears. Though we've hoped for a good ending to our wanderings, we've been easily misdirected, and the truth about who God is has been misunderstood and confused. God's character has been maligned. Alice's wonderland was full of all things nonsensical, so she questioned them. When our understanding of God and the message of the Bible don't make sense, we should question them as well. After all, her truth was fantasy; our truth is reality.

The purpose of God's election was for the temporal plan He has for the whole earth and all humanity. This is essential to where we are heading.

As Clark Pinnock observes:

> Election in the Hebrew Bible refers to God's calling of Israel as a corporate entity to service. But many would insist that the New Testament says something different, something in addition to that. They would contend that it introduces election in the sense of double predestination (where God by sovereign fiat decrees some to be saved and some to be condemned). What a tragic and influential error. The Old Testament doctrine of election remains unchanged in the New Testament. The New Testament does not reinterpret election to mean the

selection of certain individuals to be saved, leaving others aside.[85]

The Christian theological tradition on election disrupts the continuity or completely rejects it. It breaks the chain or introduces a whole new chain of ideas that are spiritual in nature, having to do with what many call *spiritual salvation* (from hell to heaven). The worst mistake of all is to force upon the idea of election, the concept that God was working to save some from hell, but not all. Just a select few. Pinnock picks up on this error when he comments on Augustine's decision to spiritualize these issues:

> It was a disaster in the history of theology when Augustine reinterpreted the biblical doctrine of election along the lines of special redemptive privilege rather than unique vocation on behalf of the world. What a mistake to have made vocational election into a soteriological category.[86]

He goes on to state rather unreservedly:

> Election has nothing to do with the eternal salvation of individuals but refers instead to God's way of saving nations. It was a major mistake of the Reformation to have decided to follow Augustine in this matter, taking election to refer to grace and salvation. It manages to make bad news out of good news. It casts a deep shadow over the character of God. At its worst, it can lead to awful consequences in terms of pride, arrogance, superiority, and intolerance as the ideology of election takes hold. It causes the church to become, not a sign of the unity of humanity in the love of God, but the sign of favorites in the midst of the enemies of God.[87]

Nothing to do with the salvation of individuals. I would venture to say if we are working with most people's definition of salvation—being saved from hell to heaven—the election purpose of God has nothing to do with this topic at all. The blessings are temporal, not eternal.

The good news is that eventually, and ultimately, God will win and establish His kingdom upon this earth. God wants all to share in this victory. This is what God has always desired and planned. He wants everyone to participate. Not all are starters. Some ride the bench while some are just fans, but God has chosen *some* in order to bless *all*. He wants all to participate in the purposes and plans for which He has created us. He wants all to share in the win. He desires that none stand in shame—believing the lie the serpent began—but that all join in the victory. He wants all to celebrate and share in His glory because all are worthy, significant, and belong.

This is how it has been since the beginning, and how it will be in the end.

Continuity from beginning to end on this most important and sensitive issue is a matter of great significance. It is a matter of truth—the truth of election and the truth of what it means to be chosen. Truth which:

- Liberates
- Dispels error
- Releases shame
- Vindicates God

This truth is that important because it influences how we understand the nature of God, His plan, and the rest of the Bible.

The Queen of Hearts was fond of proclaiming death sentences for anyone who unsettled her in any way. "Off with their heads!" was her oft-recited line. Alice first met the Queen in a garden where she witnessed card-soldiers painting white roses red. What has happened in our understanding of election is this very thing: the white roses have been painted red, perhaps not intentionally or maliciously, but nonetheless, they have been painted. Consequently, the truth obfuscated. And though it may be scary to question long-standing theologies, thankfully, there is no Queen of Hearts threatening to disconnect us from our craniums if we wash that red paint off and reveal the white rose beneath. Though there is an adversary who would much rather the white rose remain red.

This is what we find when we begin at the beginning to understand election. Election is about promised blessings for this earth, in time, for His kingdom—His real and coming kingdom. Are you starting to see the white rose emerge?

The king in *Alice's Adventure in Wonderland* said to the White Rabbit, "Begin at the beginning and go on to the end; then stop." We began at the beginning, but we are not at the end of this chain just yet. Let's press on to the end.

Follow the links in the chain, and break the bonds of shame.

---

80 Quoted at www.goodreads.com.

81 Lewis Carroll, *Alice's Adventures in Wonderland* (1865), chapter 6 Pig and Pepper.

82 Genesis 9:7 literally, to "swarm the earth."

83 Clark H. Pinnock, *A Wideness in God's Mercy*, p.23.

84 Ibid, p.25.

85 Clark H. Pinnock, *A Wideness in God's Mercy*, p.24.

86 Ibid, p.25.

87 Ibid, p.25.

Chapter 9
Broken Silence

O soul, are you weary and troubled?
No light in the darkness you see? There's light for a look at the Savior, and
life more abundant and free![88]

Even a kid who grew up on 70s and 80s rock can learn to appreciate the odes of that ol' time religion. The words above are from Helen H. Lemmel's 1922 hymn "Turn Your Eyes Upon Jesus." The truth of that stanza rings as true today as the day it was first penned. If you are weary and troubled, confused or disillusioned, there is no better place to look than Jesus. If shame is your experience and you have identified that you may have some confusion or errant beliefs about God, there is no other place and certainly no better place to look.

It is that time. Time to look to Jesus.

The Old Testament is made up of thirty-nine books, over 1,000 chapters, nearly 28,000 verses, and over 600,000 words. That's a lot of words. If you have read all or some of those words of the Old Testament and find yourself walking away scratching your head because you are not sure the assumptions and conclusions you've made or were taught make sense, you are not alone. If, when you read those ancient words, you are confused as to exactly what God is like or how you can expect Him to act, then in order to gain clarity, we can boil it down to looking at just one single word. Yes, one word: *Word*, as in "the Word became flesh and dwelt among us" (John 1:14).

This is not a new word.

This Word always existed. In fact, all things that exist came into existence through Him (John 1:1-3). That means this Word is older than any other word. This Word is not like other words that have multiple meanings and can be confusing. There are no semantics to this Word. This Word brings meaning to all significant terms and all of life, for this Word *is* life. This Word is the definitive Word about

God. This Word certainly says what we need to know to clear up any confusion we might have about the duplicitous, distorted God that has been taught to us. From the time God spoke through the last prophet (Malachi) to the time of Jesus, God was silent for over four-hundred years—no words—but now, in *The Word*, God is speaking in the Son (Hebrews 1:2). This Word, the Son, is God's way of speaking loudly, clearly, and unequivocally.

God sent Jesus, the Son, to *"explain* Him{self}*"* (John 1:18).

Here is one place a smidgen of Greek insight helps us grasp the significance of this word *explain.* In the original Greek, the word is *exēgeomai.* From it, we derive the English word *exegesis.* This may not be a term you are familiar with, but it is a term that is used in seminary circles a lot. When this word is applied to the study of literature, it means *critical explanation or interpretation of a text, esp. of Scripture.* The Greek word *exēgeomai* is a compound word made up of two Greek words: *ek,* meaning *out;* and *ēgeomai,* meaning *to lead. Exēgeomai* means "to lead out." Applied to the study of literature, it means *explain* because it is to *lead out meaning* of the text being studied. Now, connect that to the verse above. Jesus, the unique, begotten Son, is the explanation of the Father. Jesus "leads out the meaning" of the Father.

Jesus is not a correction to God in the Old Testament; He is His explanation. God does not change, and He does not talk out of both sides of His mouth.

God has not morphed into something different. He is the "I am" (Exodus 3:14). He never changes (Numbers 23:19; Malachi 3:6). There is no variation in God (James 1:17). He is immutable; the same yesterday, today, and forever (Hebrews 13:8). It is an issue of continuity.

The Son is the "exact representation of His nature" (Hebrews 1:3).

The *EXACT* representation. In other words: *what you see is what you get.*

What you see in Jesus is what you get with God. Jesus explains God. Jesus gives the old saying "the apple doesn't fall far from the tree" a whole new meaning. If you can't harmonize your understanding of God from the Old Testament with the Jesus you see in the New Testament, the problem is your understanding, *not* God.

If you can't harmonize the "truth in Jesus" (Ephesians 4:21) with the data in your head, then what is in your head is a lie or some distortion of the truth. Is God like Satan suggests, or is He like Jesus? Is the lie what we choose to believe, or is the explanation of Jesus what we trust? If our theology does not match what we see in Jesus or what we hear from His mouth (recorded in Scripture), the issue is with our theology. If this is the case, our theology needs to change so that it is consistent with what we see when we look at Jesus. And we can't (or at least we shouldn't) twist His words to fit our theology because then we bring our own meaning and place it upon the Word. That is called *eisegesis*, reading *into* the author's intended meaning another meaning instead. Sometimes our minds become so contorted after reading the words of Scripture that we are unable to read them or think about them in any way other than the way they have been taught to us. Let's open our minds and our hearts to weigh and consider freshly.

If shame is to be *damned*, we must think rightly about God and about ourselves (from His perspective). That right thinking will give us the confidence to come out from hiding in the bushes of shame, overcome fear, and engage deeply in relationship with God and others. We ought to agree with Timothy Jennings, M.D. when he writes:

> There are only two gods to be worshiped: a God of love, as revealed in Jesus, or a god that is something other than love—a being who requires some action to be taken in order to merit his mercy, forgiveness, and grace.[89]

I love the question this doctor poses after describing his own personal experience of bringing his niece and nephew to church on a Sunday when the preacher was passionately delivering a fire and brimstone sermon. Jennings asks, "Would Jesus be happy if we presented Him [God] in such a way that the children would not want to be with Him or know Him? Isn't something wrong if, in talking about God, we frighten the children?"[90] Yes, something is wrong if that is the way we think about or talk about God. Such thinking and talking are causing more problems than we are generally aware of. So we need to take another look (and listen) to Jesus.

◊137◊

Let's listen to the Word. If there is any truth to the idea of man being totally and utterly depraved, we should expect to see something to that effect from Jesus. If God is a capricious, fickle deity who picks some to love, chooses only some for heaven or relationship while choosing others to send to hell, we should expect to see something in Jesus to reinforce or reflect such a notion. Or, we might see and learn something completely different and contrary to what we have thought and what has caused so much fear and shame. Recall the song:

O soul, are you weary and troubled?
No light in the darkness you see? There's light for a look at the Savior, and
life more abundant and free!

~

Turn your eyes upon Jesus, Look full in His wonderful face,
And the things of earth will grow strangely dim,
In the light of His glory and grace.

What you see in Jesus is what you get: God. And in the words of Jesus Himself, "He who has seen Me has seen the Father" (John 14:9).

Son of Man on Man
What did Jesus say on the matter of man's condition or capacity? Does Jesus have a low view of man? Does Jesus think man is lower than pond scum? In other words, does Jesus think man is totally depraved? Damaged? Incapable of coming to or responding to God?

What is Jesus' view of man?

Did Jesus ever say or do anything that would lead us to believe He views man as damaged and completely corrupt, incapable of any good? Is man, according to Jesus, incapable of faith? Did He indicate in any of His interactions with others or His teaching that the people He was trying to reach were incapable of responding to Him? Or, is Jesus silent on the issue? Does He give us anything to help or shed light on the subject?

This little exercise is of the utmost importance because Jesus explains God. If this is who God is and how God thinks of man, we ought to expect to see it in Jesus.

In developing proper beliefs about God and man, it is never the preferred path to be argumentative, opposing, or polemic. But there is no other sound and reasonable way to be comprehensive in our battle against shame. We must be decisive and go directly to the verses that are used to buttress this errant belief. It is always preferred to be on the offensive rather than the defensive, but we all know how the enemy attacks and breaks us down. He twists Scripture to deceive and confuse. We must first untwist verses that have been twisted like pretzels and fed to us. Sometimes we need to deconstruct before we can construct.

As Paul wrote:

> For the weapons of our warfare are not of the flesh, but divinely powerful for the destruction of fortresses.[91] We are destroying speculations and every lofty thing raised up against the knowledge of God, and we are taking every thought captive to the obedience of Christ. (2 Corinthians 10:4-5)

Destruction of fortresses and speculations is necessary. This destruction is accomplished by taking our thoughts captive to Christ. Simple? Yes. Easy? That is another question altogether. Let's look at verses with the hope we can unravel our minds from errant beliefs.

To begin, we will look at a classic verse that many of the traditional perspectives use to support and defend the premise of man's utter depravity or total inability. This verse captures the very words that came out of Jesus' mouth, and it is our goal to understand them and not twist them or make them say more than He intended them to convey. The verse is John 6:44. It records Jesus as saying:

> No one can come to Me, unless the Father who sent me draws him; and I will raise him up on the last day.

If we read this verse straightforwardly, without any preconceived idea, what it says is very clear. It does not say what most people think or *make* it say. It clearly says the issue at hand is people coming to Jesus. To this, all can agree. This verse also clearly says no one is *able* to come to Jesus unless the Father draws.

This verse does *not* say:

- God only draws some.
- His drawing means man is not able (capable) within himself to come once he is drawn.
- Once drawn by God, man is not responsible to come (since he is supposed to be incapable).
- God's drawing overrides man's ability or his responsibility.

This verse *does* say:

- God draws, but man comes.
- It is man's responsibility to come. Once drawn, man is able.
- God does something to help man fulfill his responsibility, but what God does in no way excuses man's responsibility or ability.

This verse does not say everyone God draws actually comes.

So, how do so many well-intentioned students, pastors, and teachers end up with the idea that Scripture affirms man's utter depravity or total inability? What those people teach others is that man is unable to choose God unless God chooses him and draws him to Jesus. They add to this that all whom God draws will necessarily come to Him when He draws them with His "irresistible grace." God's work in drawing is so one-sided, and man's depravity so utterly complete that their coming is also attributed to God's sovereignty.

The rationale behind their conclusion is that the word *draw* means to "drag by force." With that forceful dragging in mind, many conclude it is not man's choice to come; it is God's sovereign overriding pull upon man. Many extrapolate that man does not have the capability; he is depraved and damaged. The word *draw* can certainly mean drag by force, and it is used that way in the Bible (Acts 16:19; 21:30; James 2:6), but that is not the only way, or even the most common way, the word is used.

The word is used five other times in all of the New Testament, and all five of those uses are in the gospel of John where we also find the verse under consideration. Not one of those five uses in the gospel of John clearly or necessarily means drag by force. Instead, they mean:

- *Haul,* as in haul in the nets (John 21:6, 11);
- *Unsheathe,* as in draw out one's sword (John 18:10); or, finally,
- *Draw* in the sense of attract (John 6:44; 12:32).

In all of these examples, the idea of drag by force is unnecessary and overstated. Beyond this study of the usage of this word, there are two other significant thoughts to consider. First, *if* John 6:44 means no one can come to Jesus unless God drags them by force, then John 12:32 deserves the same interpretation in its use of the word *elkō.*

In John 12:32 Jesus said, "And I, if I am lifted up from the earth, will draw all men to Myself." If the word *draw* means drag by force in John 6:44, it would be natural to interpret John 12:32 the exact same way. In fact, it would almost be necessary to do so for the sake of consistency, since the divine Being, either God the Father or Jesus, is the subject and humans are the object of the verb. If this were true, according to the view that holds to man's total inability, the point is really moot since all men will be drawn to Jesus in the end, regardless. I am not sure many who choose to interpret John 6:44 as drag by force are willing to do the same in John 12:32.[92]

The verse following John 6:44 gives us a parallel thought that ought to help us understand what Jesus most likely meant when He spoke about *drawing.* John 6:45 reads:

> It is written in the prophets, "AND THEY SHALL ALL BE TAUGHT OF GOD." Everyone who has heard and *learned* from the Father, comes to Me (italics mine).

Notice the ones who have heard and learned—who have been taught—are the ones who come to Jesus. Drawing, then, means being taught of God. Man's need for drawing from the Father does not mean man lacks the capability to hear God's voice, learn from God, or come to God. Man is not only responsible to hear, learn, and then to come (or respond to God's leading), he is also accountable for not doing so. The one who does not come does not do so because he has not heard and learned. It is not because he is incapable of doing so, and not because God has not drawn.

Notice that this word from Jesus includes a quotation from the prophets (Isaiah 54:13; Jeremiah 31:34) and was a declaration and promise for Jews. This does not mean the principle doesn't apply, but if Jesus is talking to Jews—who obviously have a history of connection with God despite being rebellious—we are not talking about "the lost" like so many people think (i.e., no knowledge of God, no faith in God, and no relationship with God). Rather, we are talking about those who do know God, yet have become *lost* like the prodigal son (Luke 15:32). What the lost sons—the lost sheep of the house of Israel—need is to come back to the Father. The way to do that is through responding to His overtures toward them: He is speaking so they will hear. He is convicting so they will learn. He is inviting them to return to His love so they may come.

What is also interesting is that in the verses to follow, His own disciples found this to be a difficult teaching to comprehend. In fact, there were some among them that did "not believe" (John 6:64). This is why Jesus turned directly to them to apply the same truth when He said, "For this reason I have said to you, that no one can come to Me unless it has been granted him from the Father." Even *disciples* need to continue to "come to Jesus." For this to happen, it must be "given" (*didōmi*) to them by the Father. Our coming to the Father is a continual and ongoing need and process.

In the Old Testament, this word *draw* is used in the Greek translation of the Hebrew Scriptures called the Septuagint[93] and is used in place of a number of different Hebrew words that have the same semantic range as *elkō* and a bit beyond. I like the picture painted in one of these places where *elkō* replaces one of the more common Hebrew words (*mashak)* in the Song of Solomon 1:4:

> Draw me after you and let us run together! The King has brought me into His chambers.

While I am more favorable to interpreting the Song of Solomon as a poem revealing God's mind and heart toward romantic relationships between a man and a woman, many understand this poem to be about God's love for humanity. Either way, it is a beautiful picture that could be comparable to Jesus' words in John 6:44 and John 12:32. God would not drag by force but might draw us through His love if we are open to learning what He is teaching.

Solomon also used the same Hebrew word in Ecclesiastes 2:3:

> I explored with my mind how to *stimulate* {Hebrew: *mashak*, translated in LXX as *elkō*} my body with wine while my mind was guiding me wisely.

This idea of stimulate as a translation of the Hebrew *mashak* corresponds nicely with *elkō* of John 6:44 which would read: "No one will come to Me unless the Father stimulate (as in draw) him." God is at work to stimulate, draw, and teach people of all sorts without distinction so they will come to Jesus to have life today and forever. The rebellious child needs drawing from God to repent. The heathen in Africa need God's drawing to be reconciled to God.

Two more verses that are commonly contorted to support these notions of man's utter inability or total depravity are John 3:3 and 3:5 which read: "Unless one is born again he cannot see" or "enter into the kingdom of God."

What do these verses say that man is *not* able to do? Respond to God? Have faith? Neither. These verses merely say man is unable to see and enter the kingdom unless he is born again. This verse does not say man is unable to meet the condition to be born again. Being born again means to be *born from above* (γεννηθη ανωθεν). In other words, to be born again is to receive life from above. The life that comes from above comes from God; it is God's life. Therefore, the birth is a spiritual birth (John 3:5), one of God's doing (John 1:13). But the condition for it to take place is man's responsibility to fulfill. If he is born again, then he has fulfilled one of the requirements for entrance into the kingdom when it is established.

Once again, when we read these verses straightforwardly, we are hard pressed to find any such notion that man is damaged and incapacitated. Instead, what we see is that there is a privilege of seeing or entering the kingdom that necessitates being born again or, more literally, being born from above. What man is unable to do is see or enter into the kingdom of God without new life, eternal life. This does not mean man lacks the ability or capacity to meet the condition—faith—in order to receive eternal life.

The condition which is upon man—any and all men—is that whoever believes may (in Him) have eternal life (John 3:15; 6:47). Man is responsible to believe because only he can do that for himself. The result of faith in Jesus is the ability to see and enter the kingdom of God. The whole process is a divine, spiritual process and can, therefore, be said to be "not of blood nor of the will of the flesh, nor of the will of man, but of God" (John 1:13). Just because God is responsible to give the life from above—to regenerate (re-birth)—it is man who must believe in order to receive.

The Verse

We need go no further to resolve many of these issues than a verse in this very same context. It is one of the best known and comprehensive verses in the Bible. Martin Luther said this one verse was the "the heart of the Bible, the gospel in miniature" because in this verse the good news is clearly and comprehensively covered. John 3:16 reads (even though you know it by heart): "For God so loved the world that He gave His only begotten Son, that whoever believes in Him shall not perish, but have eternal life."

This verse has been broken down this way:

- *God ...* The greatest Lover
- *So loved ...* The greatest degree
- *The world ...* The greatest number
- *That He gave ...* The greatest act
- *His only begotten Son ...* The greatest gift
- *That whosoever ...* The greatest invitation
- *Believeth ...* The greatest simplicity
- *In Him ...* The greatest Person
- *Should not perish ...* The greatest deliverance
- *But ...* The greatest difference
- *Have ...* The greatest certainty

- *Everlasting Life* ... The greatest possession

God loved because God *is* love, and it is even better than we might imagine: we are lovable. Just because God's love in Christ is an act of grace (unmerited favor), which we do not deserve, this does not mean we are not worthy of such love. "But God demonstrates His own love toward us, in that while we were yet sinners, Christ died for us" (Romans 5:8).

God loves the whole world. God loves universally and indiscriminately. God loves all. Jesus came for all. Jesus died for all. God loves the world. To limit the meaning of *world* to some smaller subgroup such as the elect (i.e., the ones God has chosen) is not only illogical, it is unnecessary, as we have seen in our proper understanding of election.

God loved and gave the Son so that *whosoever* would believe. We must acknowledge that God's plan is not for a select few. Neither is God's love. God loved and gave that any and all who would respond could respond, and should.

The condition that *whosoever* must meet? Believe!

Faith is the condition that rests upon man because man has the capacity to believe. In fact, man always believes something or someone. In order to see the kingdom of God, he must believe in Jesus Christ. In order to have eternal life today, he must believe in Jesus Christ. And just in case we miss the personal responsibility Jesus puts upon individuals to believe, which clearly assumes they are capable, in John 3:18 we read:

> He who believes in Him is not judged; he who does not believe has been judged already, because he has not believed in the name of the only begotten Son of God.

I don't think it takes a rocket scientist or someone with a Ph.D. to see that judgment upon man is contingent upon his faith. It would seem completely unjust to judge someone who was incapable of meeting the requirements to escape such judgment. It would not even make sense for God to act that way. In fact, it would be totally inconsistent with His nature to act so unjustly.

God Speaks, and I Like It

I know this may seem like we are engaging in debate with other perspectives and views. I am sure those who hold to views of total depravity or the utter inability of man, do so with the best of intentions and wishes, but those views are destructive to man and cause shame.

We don't need to make a man feel like pond scum—or worse than pond scum—just so he or she will appreciate the grace of God. We can be undeserving of God's grace while still being worthy of God's grace. We can be confident that we are loved and that we belong, knowing the power and capability are within us to respond to God in faith.

The good news does not need to begin so harsh and devastating. We do not need man sulking to the cross with his head hung low and "his tail between his knees." Man can stand tall and yet be humbled by the awareness of his need and the love that God has demonstrated in Jesus Christ.

You have a choice. You are capable. You are an image-bearer of God. God is good and He loves you. God considers you of immeasurable value and worth. God considers you lovable. There is no reason to fear. There is no reason to hide. There is no reason to be ashamed. Believe it. Believe Him. After 400 years of silence, God was speaking LOUD and CLEAR in His Son.

- Are you picking up what He was putting down?
- Are you seeing God for who He really is?
- Are you looking through the prism that Jesus is for us?

Build upon no other foundation than Christ; He is the perfect explanation of the Father. People's opinions are not the foundation. They are not the right material. The only solid foundation for our sense of worth, value, and lovability is Jesus Christ. It is in Him that we can find life, and life that is abundant (John 10:10).

We cannot put Jesus under the dark shadow this shameful belief of election casts, for in so doing, we rob Him of the light that He intends to shed into our hearts—light that reveals darkness and lies. Light that says, *I love you!*

Yes, you. Right where you are … YOU!

Turn your eyes upon Jesus, and come out from the bushes.

Now on to another question: Did Jesus ever specify that God only picks some?

To be continued...

---

88 Online hymnal at www.hymnal.net.

89 Timothy R. Jennings, M.D., *The God Shaped Brain*, p.66.

90 Ibid, quoted from the preface.

91 *Ochyrōma* (Greek) was a military technical term for fortified place, stronghold, bastion; figuratively in the NT as a strong system of philosophy and reasoned arguments false argument, opposed to the true knowledge of God (2C 10.4).

92 Note: to get around this obvious problem many simply redefine (i.e. limit) "all" to mean all the elect or chosen ones.

93 From the Latin word *septuaginta* meaning seventy, which was the name given to this Greek translation done by seventy Jewish scholars (2nd Century B.C.E.); the abbr. is LXX: Roman numeral for seventy.

Chapter 10
Choice Words

Clearly the person who accepts the Church as an infallible guide will believe whatever the church teaches.[94]
~ Thomas Aquinas

... Continued

I find some comfort and encouragement in knowing other people wrestle through some of the same issues I grapple with myself. In a recent blog titled *5 Reasons I reject Unconditional Election*, the words touch nerves and resonate deeply within me:

> If Christianity is worth anything at all, I must believe God is more compassionate, more merciful, more loving than I am. I refuse to redefine love to match a twisted view of God patched together from scattered Bible verses ... The only thing left to do is go back to the Scripture and read it again, differently, until I can find a God there who reflects the two truths I know to be certain: that God is like Jesus, and at the core of His being, God's essence is love. [95]

Not only do I identify with the struggle, I agree with the solution: *"... go back to the Scripture and read it again ... until I find a God who reflects the truths I know to be certain: that God is like Jesus, and the core of His being is love."* Good advice for any who, deep down, have some inclination that the God who has been taught to them does not match the divine image seen in Jesus. Maybe you are like so many other people I know who are confused and disillusioned because of how conflicting things are in mind and heart. Perhaps you are like others who are beginning to lose hope that any sense can be made of all this conflict and confusion. You may even be a little fearful to venture out and doubt, question, and wrestle.

But there is great benefit to doubt. Dallas Willard once said that we ought to believe our doubts and doubt our beliefs.[96] We learn and grow most when we are honest and authentic about our struggles, doubts, questions, and limitations. We are finite beings trying to understand the infinite. We are susceptible to being easily led astray in our finiteness to create God in our own image—messed up as that image may sometimes be. There are many explanations for why we end up holding errant beliefs. Aside from going into depth on the history of the development of beliefs and doctrines, many people understand that the historical process was anything *but* perfect or altruistic. In addition to the inherent problems arising from an imperfect process comingled with political and other convolutions of humanity, we are all subject to our social and familial dysfunctions, which seriously affect our perspectives of reality and of God. And since all families are dysfunctional at some level, we are all susceptible to some degree of distortions.

The God We Create

Psychologist Sandra D. Wilson found it is possible to predict a person's image of God from their experience of dysfunctional families who are shame-based. Interestingly, Wilson found there are "five common distortions of God's character: 1) The cruel and capricious God; 2) The demanding and unforgiving God; 3) The selective and unfair God; 4) The distant and unavailable God; 5) The kind but confused God."[97] According to Wilson's analysis and assessment, if a person grows up in an unpredictable, abusive, rigid, perfectionistic, demanding, unforgiving, unfair, or chaotic, dysfunctional family, there is a high likelihood that once they become adults, they will hold some dysfunctional distortions of God's character. If these terms do not describe your experience with pinpoint accuracy, surely some of them hit close to home.

- Unpredictable
- Rigid
- Performance-driven
- Unfair

- Abusive
- Chaotic

Wilson calls the "selective and unfair" distortion of God the "epitome of a shame-shaped deity."[98] A selective and unfair God plays favorites and is only "cruel, capricious, demanding, and unforgiving" to those who don't bow before Him. God, in this distortion, is a picky God who only loves the ones worthy of love—certainly not the unlovable, less fortunate, hurting, and downcast of society. What effect do these kinds of distortions have on us? They lead us to live confused, fearful, and shame-riddled lives—if you can call that living. This is why, as Wilson writes, "Correcting distorted concepts of God is arguably the most important aspect of the lifelong process of mind renewal by which we, as Christians, are being continually transformed."[99] It is no wonder God would inspire Paul to write to the Romans:

> And do not be conformed to this world, but be transformed by the renewing of your mind, so that you may prove what the will of God is, that which is good and acceptable and perfect. (Romans 12:2).

Dallas Willard often said this word *world* is simply the way most people think.[100] We need to stop being conformed to how others think. We need to correct any and all distortions of God, especially ones that cause shame. We need to go back to the Bible to see if God is really like our theology or if He's more like Jesus. If the God we see revealed in Jesus does not match the God of our theology, we need to stop being conformed and be renewed in our minds.

Is Jesus like this *epitome of a shame-shaped deity*? Does He show favorites, thinking only some are worthy of love while others are not? Is Jesus discriminating and persnickety? Is He unpredictable? Does Jesus choose some for heaven and others for an eternity in hell by passing over them or not choosing them? Does He believe in unconditional election?

Or ...

Is Jesus more faithful, merciful, and compassionate than we have been taught or ever imagined?

Is Jesus more loving, merciful, and forgiving than I am?

The words of Jesus have been so twisted and contorted that the picture of Him doesn't accurately reflect who He really is. In fact, at times He seems unrecognizable. We need to unravel His words so we can be renewed in our minds and understand Him properly. The Jesus who has been taught to us and handed down from well-intentioned men and women of church history is a distortion of the real Jesus.

Counselor and interventionist Jeff VanVonderen is, by his own admission, no stranger to shame. He found after years of counseling people who struggled with shame: "More often than not, the spiritual issue with which my clients struggle isn't a question of *whether* or not there is a God. It's a matter of fearing that there is."[101]

Fearful that God exists. Do you see a problem here? VanVonderen goes on to explain how this fearing of the existence of God is due to how God had been represented to them by those who bear His name. A pattern has been emerging along this line for many, many years. Distortions of God as a shame-shaped deity are not helping anyone. The pain-ridden voices all around us are crying out—unless it is too late and they have gone silent. We must stop with the distorted God-concepts.

Let's go back to the source. Jesus is *the* Chosen One (Matthew 12:18; Luke 9:35; 23:35) so what does He say about choosing?

To begin, we must understand the mission of Jesus Christ.

Man on a Mission

We can get a good grasp of Jesus' mission if we listen to God speak.

After four hundred years of silence, just as He told the prophet Malachi, God sent Elijah the prophet as a precursor to God's redemption (Malachi 4:5). When we open the pages of the New Testament, we find God making good on His promises. The angel Gabriel told a priest named Zacharias his son would "turn many of the sons of Israel back to the Lord their God ... as a forerunner before Him in the spirit and power of Elijah, 'TO TURN THE HEARTS OF THE FATHERS BACK TO THE CHILDREN,' and the disobedient to the attitude of the righteous; so as to make ready a people prepared for the Lord" (Luke 1:16-17). It was a sign of Messianic times. God was moving again toward the nation of Israel to whom He had promised deliverance, but the first step was for their hearts to be turned away from *whatever* and back to God.

The angel Gabriel also came to a virgin named Mary to inform her that she, like her cousin Elizabeth, would conceive a child whom she was to name Jesus (lit., Yahweh saves) and he would "be great, and will be called the Son of the Most High, and the Lord God will give Him the throne of His father David; and He will reign over the house of Jacob forever and His kingdom will have no end" (Luke 1:32-33). Jesus, born to a virgin and to a less than significant carpenter of Nazareth, would be King and sit on the throne of David. His reign would be over the nation of Israel and upon this earth.

Zacharias (the priest and father of John the Baptist) was "filled with the Holy Spirit, and prophesied" (Luke 1:67) about the Messianic hope, deliverance of God's people, Israel, and God's faithfulness to the covenant He made to Abraham (Luke 1:68-79). This mission was not a new mission or new religion; it was a continuation of God's movement and mission that began in the Garden of Eden and was carried though the history of the Old Testament. God was moving again with the promise to establish a kingdom through Israel, the chosen nation, through the Anointed One: the Christ.

This is the mission of God and the mission of Messiah: Jesus Christ.

When God spoke to the shepherds, He said, "I bring you good news of great joy which shall be for all people; for today in the city of David there has been born for you a Savior, who is Christ the Lord" (Luke 2:10-11).

- There has been born for you a *Savior*.
- Good news for *all* people.
- Great joy for *all* people.

God had been speaking to an older man named Simeon (Luke 2:26) who was a righteous and devout man, "looking for the consolation of Israel; and the Holy Spirit was upon him" (Luke 2:25). When Simeon saw the baby Jesus, he said, "For my eyes have seen Your salvation, which You have prepared in the presence of all peoples, 'A LIGHT OF

REVELATION TO THE GENTILES,' and the glory of Your people Israel" (Luke 2:30-32). Don't miss what was being said. God had a mission and a plan. His plan was first for Israel, but would include everyone.

God elected Jesus to come first for His chosen people, Israel, so He could use them to shed light to the whole world. This has always been and remains the plan. This is why Jesus could say, "I was sent only to the lost sheep of the house of Israel" (Matthew 15:24). Israel will always have first crack at being the vehicle through which God will bless the whole earth and restore all things back to His original purpose and plan. The nation of Israel, the physical descendants of Abraham, Isaac, and Jacob, are God's *elect* (Matthew 24:22, 24, 31; Mark 13:20, 22, 27; Luke 18:7), chosen vessels to accomplish His plans for the whole world. Israel was chosen to serve.

God's plan in Jesus was "for all the fullness to dwell in Him, and through Him to reconcile all things to Himself" (Colossians 1:19-20). It started with the nation God chose to serve Him in antiquity: Israel.

God's promises to Israel came with conditions. The nation had to be humble and righteous. That is why Jesus' message began with the word "repent." Israel had to change their minds about God and themselves before God would fulfill His promises to them.

His mission was to set up a kingdom for a righteous people who, in turn, He could use to reach the world. The kingdom is how God will get hell out of earth, not get us out of hell. This is the reason He came, and the reason He will come again.

But first things first.

Rejected yet Not Alone

The apostle John summed up the story of the first coming of Messiah Jesus: "In Him was life, and the life was the light of men. The light shines in the darkness, and the darkness did not comprehend it" (John 1:4-5).

There was the true light which, coming into the world, enlightens every man. He was in the world, and the world was made through Him, and the world did not know Him. He came to His own, and those who were His own did not receive Him (John 1:9-11).

Israel built up what could be seen as a huge shame defense system. They had become self-righteous. Believing they were victims, they were confident God owed the promises to them simply because of their DNA. As a nation, they were no longer able or willing to see their own darkness.

But God has a way of making beauty out of our *ugly*.

John, after penning, "His own did not receive Him," wrote that in contrast to the unreceptive nation, there was still a glimmer of hope for people: "But as many as received Him, to them He gave the right to become children of God, even to those who believe in His name, who were born not of blood, nor of the will of the flesh, nor of the will of man, but of God" (John 1:12-13).

His own, the chosen nation to which He came, did not receive Him. But many individuals did, and some of those were Gentiles. As a result of the nation's rejection, a mystery was revealed that any and all who responded faithfully to Jesus and His message were put in the position of being children of God. This is very similar to the picture of Jacob making Joseph's sons, Ephraim and Manasseh, his own children, even though they were already a part of the family. As his grandchildren, they would enjoy the blessings when fulfilled. But children have rights that grandchildren don't. Children have first right to the riches and inheritance of the father. This is the idea of adoption as sons in the Bible: Gentiles being placed in the position of the firstborns and their privileges to inheritance (Romans 8:15, 23; Galatians 3:23-4:5; Ephesians 1:5).

Jesus gave us a number of wonderful little sneak peeks, or previews, of this great new development. The preview we see in Jesus will be of a mystery that will later be unfolded in great detail through the apostle Paul.

The Real Jesus

Take a look at a few of those little previews. Any distortions or misunderstandings you might have about Jesus should begin to be corrected.

The first sneak peek was exactly what happened one day—somewhere around A.D. 30—in a town named Capernaum. This is a story of a Gentile coming to Jesus (Matthew 8:5-13). Jesus came for Israel, and yet Gentiles came to Jesus. This man was not of the favored and chosen nation. This man had no history or connection to the promises of God made to Abraham, Isaac, Jacob, or David. But this man was desperate. This man was needy. This Gentile came to Jesus to ask for a favor (8:5). He came asking for help. It might even be fair to say he came begging for divine intervention. You see, this man's son was sick. It was more serious than a common cold or the flu; this man's son was unable to walk and was in torment and pain (8:6).

Did Jesus turn him away since he was not of the *chosen* nation? No. Jesus agreed to come and heal him (8:7). Just what we might expect from God.

But there was a problem. The Centurion knew where he ranked in the religious order of merit. He said to Jesus, "Lord, I am not worthy for You to come under my roof" (8:9a). This Gentile had a mixture of truth and fiction, and of right thinking and distortion. He knew Jesus was able, but he doubted his own worth.

This Gentile was a commander of one hundred soldiers. He was a Roman and—at the time—the Romans had made Israel their errand boy. Yet, he was a good man. Luke tells us the Jewish elders (whom the man sent to represent him the first time) told Jesus this Centurion loved the Jews and even built them a synagogue to worship in (Luke 7:5). He was not like so many other Gentile rulers who were mean-spirited, dominating, demeaning, and dictatorial (Matthew 20:25; Mark 10:42; Luke 22:25). He was a good man and a generous, caring, and kind leader. But this man knew where he stood since he knew Jesus came for the Jews. One way or another, he thought he was not worthy.

But Jesus thought otherwise.

This Gentile man was a man of faith, "great faith" according to Jesus (Matthew 8:10). In fact, the faith this man exhibited was greater than any faith Jesus had found thus far in the chosen nation of Israel for which He came. This faith—the faith of a Gentile—is what prompted Jesus to give us the sneak peek of what blessings would be opened up to Gentiles.

Was this man a believer? Was this man going to heaven if he died? Yes and yes, but so much more is put on the table for us to consider.

This man was going to "recline at the table with Abraham, and Isaac, and Jacob, in the kingdom of heaven; but the sons of the kingdom would be cast out" (Matthew 8:11-12). In short, Jesus was saying this man, a Gentile, was going to experience the blessings of participating in the coming kingdom with its celebrations, blessings, and privileges, all of which were originally promised first to the chosen nation of Israel, God's first-born.

This Gentile, although not part of the chosen nation, was a believing and willing servant of Yahweh and Jesus. It is upon this basis that he is promised these great blessings and rewards in the coming kingdom of Messiah. While Jesus came for the lost sheep of the house of Israel to establish His kingdom, God is not unfair and selective in His love, grace, and mercy. This ought to help us unravel any distortions we have about Jesus picking some and not others.

A Gentile with "great faith" was welcomed with open arms by Jesus.

Great faith. Great news.

The only other occasion of Jesus recognizing great faith came in His brief dealings with a Canaanite woman (Matthew 15:21-28). A Canaanite—thus another Gentile—and a woman, no less. She came to Him for mercy because her daughter was being tormented by a demon. His disciples were having nothing of the distraction and possible diversion from their mission. Jesus' first response was a reminder of His primary purpose: "I was sent only to the lost sheep of the house of Israel" (Matthew 15:24). The Canaanite woman was undeterred. She bowed down before Him in worship and pled for help. Jesus reminded the woman that what He had to offer was not for Gentiles as a matter of priority. But the woman was faithfully persistent and humble. She knew she could survive on the crumbs that fell from the table. That's when Jesus said it: "Your faith is great." He healed her daughter immediately.

Another sneak peek of what was to come. Another clue in the story that helps us untwist the twisted Jesus.

Twisted Words Untangled

I have shared this perspective of God's comprehensive love with many people along the way. One response I often get that is typical of the thinking of so many is this: "Didn't Jesus say many are called but few are chosen?" The answer is yes, but that does not mean what we have contorted it to mean. Let's take a look.

The verse that many think indicates Jesus believed in unconditional election is Matthew 22:14 which says, "many are called but few are chosen."

On the surface, it is easy to see how this verse could be mistaken to say something it doesn't, even though heaven and hell are not mentioned. If, however, a person reads the whole parable and the context in which this verse was originally given, a completely different understanding emerges.

Jesus saw very early-on the problem of Israel's rejection of Him and His offer of the kingdom, and He began to announce His rejection and death. As the day of His rejection grew near, there was a noticeable shift in the nature of His message. It was "the kingdom of heaven is at hand," and it turned into a message about the king going away (Luke 19:12; Matthew 25:14-31). When Jesus was just an infant, godly people like Simeon knew the plan would be a bit messy. Simeon told Mary, "… this Child is appointed for the fall and rise of many in Israel, and for a sign to be opposed—and a sword will pierce even your own soul—to the end that thoughts from many hearts may be revealed" (Luke 2:34-35). God's plan to establish His kingdom upon the earth would involve the suffering of His Anointed (Isaiah 53) at the hands of the very nation He came to rescue. This plan was a "predetermined plan" (Acts 2:23). This suffering of Messiah revealed in the Old Testament (Isaiah 53 or Zechariah 9) was misunderstood by the majority of the nation of Israel. In fact, so confused were some by the two vastly different pictures of Messiah in the Old Testament, many thought there would be two Messiahs: one like Joseph and the other like David.[102]

As a result of the rejection by the nation, Jesus began teaching that the kingdom was going to be postponed until a time when a generation of the chosen nation would respond righteously (Matthew 21:43). Despite the fact that the kingdom promises would be postponed, in the meantime God was going to continue to do a mighty work to use people to shed His light. Those who would respond to Him and faithfully serve Him during this time would inherit great riches, rewards, and responsibility in the coming kingdom when it is established.

In light of His rejection by the nation, Jesus started to teach differently, especially in parables. In Matthew 22:1-14, where we find the verse under consideration, is a parable called the "parable of the wedding feast."

Context, context, context: the three most important rules in interpretation.

Jesus had just told the chief priests and the elders of the people and the Pharisees (Matthew 21:23, 45) through a parable (Matthew 21:31-34) and then directly (Matthew 21:42-44) that the kingdom, which He had been offering to the nation, would be "taken away from you and given to a people, producing the fruit of it" (Matthew 21:43). The leaders of the nation of Israel understood that He was talking about them, and they really wanted to throw Him into jail right then (21:45). That is when Jesus spoke to them again in a parable: "The kingdom of heaven[103] may be compared to a king who gave a wedding feast for his son" (Matthew 22:1-2).

It is of the utmost importance not to make the same mistake so many have made by thinking the kingdom of heaven is actually the same thing as getting to go to heaven when we die. The two are not the same. The kingdom of heaven is a kingdom for earth and will take place on earth even though it is not of the world. It is not like worldly kingdoms that are imperfect. I have written more extensively on this very matter in *Majestic Destiny: Kingdom Hope is Rising*.

You can read the parable for yourself, but let me summarize. It is about the kingdom plan for this earth, which is promised to the nation of Israel. This kingdom, which has been adequately offered to the nation, is being postponed (*taken*) and will be given to a generation of that nation producing the fruit of it (i.e., the "fruit worthy of repentance," Matthew 3:8; Luke 3:8). As Paul writes: "A partial hardening has happened to Israel until the fullness of the Gentiles has come in; and so all Israel will be saved; just as it is written" (Romans 11:25-26). A remnant of Israel will repent and turn their hearts back to God. And God will be faithful to Israel in the future because "the gifts and the calling of God are irrevocable" (Romans 11:29).

In the parable, the king sends out slaves to call those who had been invited (Matthew 22:3). If the parable coincided with a historical situation at the time, this would coincide with the invitation Jesus and His disciples were giving to the nation of Israel. But Israel was "unwilling to come" (Matthew 22:3). Longsuffering as He is, He sends out another call, but "they paid no attention and went their way" (Matthew 22:5). Worse yet, they resorted to violence (Matthew 22:6). This may be a prophetic picture of what would take place through the Acts of the Apostles (see the whole book of Acts). As a result of their violence against the king's servants, those invited suffered chastisement (Matthew 22:7). Many people see this as a prophecy of the destruction that would come upon Israel at the hands of the Romans—a historically undeniable fact (A.D. 70 at the hands of emperor Titus Flavius).

Since the first group of invitees did not respond to the call because they were not worthy (since their hearts were hard), a new invitation went out to "as many as you find" (Matthew 22:9) without regard to previous standing. This closely parallels what is recorded in the progression of the good news in the book of Acts (started with messages to Jews but then taken to Gentiles). As a result of this broadened invitation, people came, and the "wedding hall was filled with dinner guests" (Matthew 22:10).

One might think this would be a nice ending to the story, but then something curious happens. One of the invited guests has not properly attired himself for the occasion. When the king comes to the banquet and sees the man, the king inquires of this "friend" (Matthew 22:12). Getting no response from the shabbily dressed man, the king orders his slaves to put the man outside of the celebration. Then Jesus gives this explanation to the parable: "For many are called {or invited}, but few are chosen" (Matthew 22:14).

This explanation may be longer than you were looking for, so I will try to wrap it up. This is important and makes a difference.

What is interesting in this misunderstood verse is that the words translated *called* and *chosen* are not verbs, they are adjectives. So instead of translating them as action words (verbs), they should be translated as adjectives. If you receive an invitation, you are an *invitee*.

If you are well dressed (i.e., prepared), you are *choice*. Interpreting and translating the word *eklegō* (to choose) as an adjective communicates the qualitative nature of the word and not the action of someone choosing or the person chosen. It is like superior, best, first-rate. If you buy beef in the butcher shop, you might see a stamp on the package that reads "Choice Beef," which indicates the grade of the meat is between prime and good.

The gentleman in the parable was not appropriately attired. He was not *choice* because he had not done what was necessary to prepare himself for such a first-rate experience. While the invitation went out to many, it is assumed that those who received the invitation all understood the conditions necessary for participation—except this man. The point is that many are invited to participate in the kingdom, especially since the nation rejected His offer, yet the same conditions apply to the new group of invitees as applied to the nation. They must be worthy, bring forth fruits worthy of repentance, in keeping with repentance. They must be *choice*.

I think the Pharisees and other religious leaders got the picture, for after hearing this parable they "plotted together how they might trap Him in what He said" (Matthew 22:15).

This verse, which has been twisted and made nearly unrecognizable in relation to its original intent, is not about Jesus inviting many to heaven and yet choosing only a few that will actually get to go. That is a distortion of the true God revealed in Jesus.

Once we have a different way to understand these passages which is consistent with the context, we are that much closer.

But we are not there yet.

Other Distortions

Our well-intentioned spiritual family, the church, has twisted some other verses that conjure up a picture of Jesus that does not match the general picture of Him in the gospels and what we know in our hearts to be true.

Maybe you have heard someone quote Jesus' words when He said He "gives life to whom He wishes" (John 5:21). In addition to the quote, they might offer an interpretation of these words to mean Jesus doesn't wish to give life to all but only a select few. Some will say this proves Jesus agreed with the doctrine of unconditional election, but it really does not prove that at all. In this verse (John 5:21), Jesus gave life to an undesirable of his day, a crippled man. But it happened to be on the Sabbath, which irritated the religious elite. Jesus told them He was God and because He was, He could give life to *anyone* He wishes *whenever* He wishes. This does not mean He does not wish to give life to everyone. We know God "desires all men to be saved" (1 Timothy 2:4) which would seem to clearly contradict such an idea. Also, we know God "is patient toward you, not wishing for any to perish but for all to come to repentance" (2 Peter 3:9). Once again, this seems to clearly contradict such an idea that God is only interested in giving life to a select few.

We cannot confuse what took place in a moment in time with God's universal plan for all moments and all people.

Seeing Clearly

Henri Nouwen once wrote that "Jesus is the revelation of God's unending, unconditional love for us human beings. Everything that Jesus has done, said, and undergone is meant to show us that the love we most long for is given to us by God—not because we've deserved it, but because God is a God of love."[104]

What does Jesus show us? That God is selective and unfair?

Does Jesus resemble a shame-shaped deity?

Or ...is Jesus more loving than I am? Is Jesus more loving than any of us?

Have we misunderstood and twisted the words of the Bible with the result being a perspective of God that is unfair and selective? We need to unravel what has been raveled. Jesus never gave any indication that He believed in selecting a limited number of people to which He was willing to show His love and grace—while others He ignored, refused, or denied the same. Jesus chose those whom He would use, but this is very different from saying Jesus chose some for heaven and others He destined to hell.

There is no hint of unconditional election in anything Jesus said or did. Jesus did not believe in unconditional election because such an idea is a distortion of who God is. I like how the late Clark Pinnock put it: "God sent Jesus to be the Savior of the world, not the Savior of a select few. This fact empowers us to approach all persons in a spirit of openness and love. It fills us with optimism and expectation because we know what God is aiming at."[105]

The gates of God's grace and love are open wide in the arms of Jesus. There is no such thing as a person who is "born to lose," for all are born to love and be loved. God does not have a list of those whom He has chosen to be loved, for God loves the whole world. Just ask Jesus. After His death, He redirected the focus of the disciples. And guess what? Now they would expand their territories. Now, all nations would be brought to God through Jesus. Jesus said, "Go, therefore, and make disciples of all the nations..." (Matthew 28:19).

As Luke records, Jesus said, "Repentance for forgiveness of sins would be proclaimed in His name to all nations" (Luke 24:47).

After His death, Jesus told His disciples they would be His witnesses "even to the remotest part of the earth" (Acts 1:8).

Jesus flung open God's everlasting lovingkindness by stretching out His arms upon the cross. He bore our shame and grief as a suffering servant (Isaiah 53). He took our shame. In the words of the author of the book of Hebrews, "... who for the joy set before Him endured the cross, despising the shame ..." (Hebrews 12:2). Jesus is not a shame-shaped deity. Jesus took shame head-on. He despised shame for you and me. Jesus doesn't duck shame; He destroys it. Shame disintegrates in the presence of Jesus.

We are all naked, spiritually speaking. Thus, we need to be clothed. And we have the perfect suit for the occasion. Once again, as He was with Adam and Eve, God is our tailor.

This time, the suit is not fig leaves or animal skins. Paul wrote, "For all of you who were baptized into Christ have clothed yourselves with Christ" (Galatians 3:27). Clothed with Christ. Clothed with God Himself. What a covering.

To be clothed in Christ is to be shameless.

Don't listen to anything or anyone else. The only way to experience the life He came to give, leaving shame far behind, is to put on the

Jesus revealed, not some unrecognizable version of Him we have been taught by others.

Put on Christ and follow Him.

94 Quoted from http://www.brainyquote.com/quotes/quotes/t/thomasaqui1869-09.html.

95 Dallas Willard, video recording on What Skepticism Is Good For, Claremont Consortium (2013).

96 Dallas Willard, video recording on What Skepticism Is Good For, Claremont Consortium (2013).

97 Sandra D. Wilson, *Released from Shame: Recovery for Adult Children of Dysfunctional Families*, pp.150-1.

98 Ibid., p.150.

99 Ibid., p.151.

100 Quoted from www.dallaswillard.org.

101 Jeff VanVonderen, *Tired of Trying to Measure Up*, p. 78.

102 See the articles at www.jewsforjesus.org/publications/issues/v15-n05/returningking www.jewishroots.net/library/messianic/two-messiahs.

103 The kingdom of heaven is not heaven itself, but a kingdom that is other worldly (John 18:36) and will come down from heaven like a rock described by Daniel (Daniel 2:34-35; 44-45) to destroy all the other kingdoms of this world. This is the kingdom of Messiah on this earth.

104 Henri Nouwen, *Letters To Marc About Jesus*, (Kindle Locations 756-758) HarperCollins, Kindle Edition.

105 Clark Pinnock, *A Wideness in God's Mercy*, p.47.

Chapter 11
Beauty, the Beast, and da Hawaiian Guy

Those who find ugly meanings in beautiful things are corrupt without being charming.
~ Oscar Wilde[106]

Who doesn't like a good story of transformation from ugly duckling to beautiful swan?

- Raggedy maid to beautiful princess.
- Toad to prince.
- Beast to handsome prince charming.

While all of these stories and fables have lasting qualities, one cannot deny the masterful and poetic splendor of *Beauty and the Beast*. This enduring story has resonated in the minds and hearts of millions since it was written in 1756 by Jeanne-Marie Leprince de Beaumont. This story is definitely the stuff of Hollywood movies. Made into a movie numerous times, the most well-known is Walt Disney's 1991 animation production. Stories of transformation capture our interest and continually excite and amaze us: a dying beast, breathing what could be his last breath, transformed back into a handsome, charming prince by the tear of a beautiful young lady all because of love. That never gets old.

Beast to beauty.

Sometimes words get twisted to mean something the author or speaker never intended. When words get misrepresented, taken out of context, or misunderstood, it is the person who supposedly spoke them who gets maligned and turned into a beast. I am sure all of us at one time or another have said something that someone took completely wrong and possibly shared it with others, putting us in a bad light. To make something ugly because of confusion, misunderstanding, or because words were taken completely out of context is very frustrating. That is why the Bible is so clear on prohibition against slander and gossip. Sometimes it is simply an issue of misunderstanding. Sometimes it is an issue of misquoting. At other times, it is nothing less than misrepresentation. This is how someone can take something like your words and make you out to be a beast. To turn the beast back to the beauty, the misunderstanding, misquoting, or misrepresentation must be dealt with.

This same phenomenon happens with the Word of God.

A Daily Dose

Hopefully by now—if you have lived in fear and hiding, unaware you are worthy and lovable—the "good news" is becoming something that really feels and sounds like good news. But just because you are getting a flavor of shamelessness today does not guarantee it will automatically taste the same tomorrow. Shamelessness is a daily endeavor. Living free and out of hiding will be an ongoing process and journey you must prepare, plan, and purpose to live each day. If you fail to prepare, plan, and purpose, it is easy to slip back into shame ... back into the bushes. Shamelessness on Monday is no guarantee of the same on Tuesday.

And here is how it slips out of our fingers.

Life is full of problems and negative voices lurking behind every corner. This world is under the authority of an adversary who prefers we live in hiding and shame. He is prowling and seeking to devour (1 Peter 5:8). One of his favorite methods of trying to destroy our authentic, wholehearted, shameless living is to twist God's Word to contradict what we know to be true about ourselves and our Father. He tried the very same thing on Jesus, albeit unsuccessfully (Matthew 4:5-7). This adversary is incredibly sneaky and sly when it comes to his attack on us and our shame-free living. This is why, to be prepared, we must look at other passages in the Bible that have been twisted time and time again, contorting our perspective of God.

We have already seen that there are different ways, more positive ways, to view the verses that have been used to develop a low view of man as damaged, dead, and damned. We have untwisted those verses that were twisted beyond recognition. We saw how many of the verses commonly used to paint Jesus as a random, selective, and unfair God who picks and chooses who goes to heaven and who goes to hell, can and should be viewed in a different light. These different perspectives and interpretations fit nicely into the overall story of the Bible and don't contradict what we instinctively know about God.

We must now look at other verses that have been misquoted, misunderstood, and misrepresent God. As you weigh and consider new ways to understand these verses, you are preparing by building a shame defense system. We don't need to kiss a frog or shed a tear to uncover the beauty. We must peel back the theology and look at these verses to see if there is another way to understand them, one that is consistent with the God we see revealed in the Bible and which resonates deeply in our heart and soul. Our job is to thoughtfully and prayerfully weigh and consider proposed perspectives of the truth.

If we turn down the noise of our lives and think deeply, honestly, and humbly about these truths, they will likely take root in our souls and free us from any remaining errant beliefs about God and the consequent shame that may exist as a result of those errant beliefs. These new perspectives and alternative ways to consider verses will hopefully show how the misunderstandings have made these verses beastly, but reveal them as something beautiful.

Beast to beauty. What we will find is the beauty we seek and long for was there all along. It is a love story, a story of beauty and mystery. Let's take a look.

The Mystery

God is a lover. We are His beloved. And so is the whole world.

Always has been this way and always will be.

But God's romance with the world does not always go as planned—no fault of God's, of course. God has often been the jilted lover. In the book of Hosea, His relationship with Israel is paralleled by Hosea's relationship with a promiscuous woman named Gomer. As Gomer jilts Hosea and returns to the streets and a life of harlotry, so does Israel jilt God, leaving Him for other gods. Israel dumped God many times and played the harlot. But God is not like a normal lover. While God has been jilted many times, His lovingkindness is everlasting (see Psalm 136 for an example).

In the book of Hosea, God compares His relationship with Israel to that of Hosea, who goes looking for his wife. He waits and watches for her so he may find her and bring her home. His lovingkindness is everlasting. The Bible is a love story that unfolds that drama.

When Jesus began his ministry, He came lovingly to this disobedient people, the lost sheep of the house of Israel, calling them to repentance—to change their mind and get back on track with their God. He did this because His lovingkindness is everlasting. The nation of Israel, however, rejected Jesus' offer because they did not like the conditions that He said were absolutely necessary, namely repentance. The nation misunderstood God's kindness and became a self-righteous people who saw no need for repentance. God's kindness, however, should always be understood to lead to repentance (Romans 2:4). Israel's status, position, and calling, as God's chosen, went to their heads. They became an ostracizing and exclusivist nation, not a light-bearing nation, which was God's desire. They shunned rather than shined.

Jesus made it clear this was a serious problem when He said, "But woe to you scribes and Pharisees, hypocrites, because you shut off the kingdom of heaven from people; for you do not enter in yourselves, nor do you allow those who are entering to go in" (Matthew 23:13).

Religion, when it loses sight of the mission and heart of God, tends to be exclusivistic. Putting other people below us is oftentimes our best attempt to cover up our own shame. This is exactly the heart of what psychiatrist Peter Loader is getting at when he states that people cover up or compensate for deep feelings of shame with attitudes of contempt, superiority, domineering or bullying, self-deprecation, or obsessive perfectionism.[107] This was the state of mind of Israel at the time Jesus came. They were better than everyone else. They were superior. They domineered and bullied. They were obsessively perfectionistic. This undoubtedly was driven by shame. As a result, they were unable, not just unwilling, to recognize their need for repentance. So once again, they jilted the Lover; only this time they put Him upon a cross on a hill called Calvary.

What happens when a lover is jilted by her beloved? Either the lover refuses to be near to the beloved—absence makes the heart grow fonder—or the lover releases him and lets him go his own way in hopes that he will figure out on his own how much better it is to be with his lover. God used both of these tactics in the history of Israel. Now God would try a new tactic to bring His beloved back. This time the strategy would be jealousy.

Again, we return to the book of Hosea for a telling picture.

Israel dumped God on many occasions. As a result, God would withdraw His presence from them or remove them from a position of blessing, specifically the Land of Promise. The prophetic picture in Hosea is of God giving Israel a certificate of divorce. Yet, in the end, it is clear all these actions are governed by love and a desire to win back His people. He acted in such ways, as a jilted lover, to provoke in them a jealousy that would move them back to intimacy with their husband. We read in Hosea that God's desire is and always will be to restore people to harmony with Him so He can bless them (see Hosea 2:14-23, the remarriage of Israel to God). This idea of reconciliation and reunification is clearly taught in Hosea 2:23 when God said, "I will sow her for Myself in the land. I will also have compassion on her who had not obtained compassion, and I will say to those who were not My people, 'You are my people!' And they will say, 'You are my God!'" What is most interesting is that both Paul and Peter apply this verse to the church (Romans 9:25; 1 Peter 2:10).

Why or how might we understand this verse applying to the church? God has invited the church, a non-nationalistic organism made up of Jew and Gentile, into the love triangle to mix it up and move the nation of Israel to jealousy. He "is the same yesterday and today and forever" (Hebrews 13:8), yet He often surprises us.

One of the surprising purposes for the church made up of both Jew *and Gentile*—and reasons the church has been chosen and called by God to serve Him and have the possibility of great blessings—is "to make them [Israel] jealous" (Romans 11:11). God had forewarned Israel of this potential if they were not faithful to Him (Romans 10:19 quoting Deuteronomy 32:21).

Jealousy is not *all* bad.[108]

God is a jealous God (Exodus 20:4-5; 34:14; Deuteronomy 6:15). When the Bible speaks about God as jealous, it means He is zealous for His creatures because of His love.

- He is jealous for a people for His own possession (Zechariah 1:14; 8:2).
- He jealously desires the Spirit He has made to dwell in us (James 4:5).
- He wants all men to be saved (1 Timothy 2:4). He does not want any to perish (2 Peter 3:9).

In the Song of Solomon, romantic love is said to be "as strong as death; jealousy is as severe as Sheol. Its flashes are flashes of fire, the very flame of the Lord" (Song of Solomon 8:6-7). Our love for a spouse is compared to God's love, a jealous, fiery love.

Jealousy, in this context, is good.

The only sensible reason God would purposefully stir up and wish to incite jealousy is so the nation would return to their jilted Lover. And they will. The church's job is to make that as easy as possible. It is our time to shine.

Paul makes sure the church—especially Gentiles—does not let this newly discovered position of service and glory go to their heads so they become wise in their own estimation (Romans 11:25). The priority of position the church finds itself in, by the grace of God, is not going to go on forever because "a partial hardening has happened to Israel *until* the fullness of the Gentiles has come in" (Romans 11:25b). This means Israel's hard heart, rebellion, and rejection of Jesus won't last forever. In the end, "all Israel will be saved" (Romans 11:26).

This is a good thing because we need Israel to get grafted back in order for God to fulfill His promise to them so that we also might share in it. The salvation spoken of in Romans is not deliverance from hell, but redemption for the earth and God's people. This salvation is "nearer to us than when we believed" (Romans 13:11). It is the salvation that will come with the return of Jesus Christ "without reference to sin" (Hebrews 9:28).

Israel will be moved by jealousy and will one day "call upon the Lord and be saved" (Romans 10:13; Joel 2:32), even though it will only come after great tribulation (see Daniel's prophecies of the seventy weeks). Make no mistake, though. God will fulfill every promise to Israel for "the gifts and the calling of God are irrevocable" (Romans 11:29). God cannot change His mind. God's promises to Israel are like an irrevocable trust. Even though it is the Church's time to shine and will share in the privileges and promises, Israel will still get theirs. It is just sitting in a trust account.

Israel will be shown mercy (Romans 11:31) as He is now showing to all (Romans 11:32). Israel will shine and nations will come to their light (Isaiah 60:1-3; Daniel 12:3).

But until that day, it is our time to shine.

Beastly ... not. Beauty.

More Beauty

One passage has been turned into a beast, creating a beastly image of God. But the reality is that beauty exists and has been there all along. Let's seek for beauty together in these ancient words.

Ephesians 1:4-5 reads:

> Just as He chose us in Him before the foundation of the world, that we would be holy and blameless before Him. In love He predestined us to adoption as sons through Jesus Christ to Himself, according to the kind intention of His will.

Some very important words here:

- Chose
- Predestined

Sound familiar? Keeping what we've already talked about in mind, you can imagine how this verse gets all twisted around. As a result, God comes out looking more like a beast than a loving prince. What has typically and traditionally been said of these verses is that God chooses before the foundation of the world those who will believe in Jesus and go to heaven when they die. This choosing, according to most of this perspective, determines who will actually believe while others—*not chosen*—never have the chance at faith and redemption.

This traditional interpretation and understanding take us right back to a picture of God that, quite frankly, can't be trusted. There are all sorts of potential problems and pitfalls awaiting this understanding of God. This perspective of God, based on this verse and a couple others like it, lead many to believe God is duplicitous and selective in His love and, therefore, in our perceived lovability or worth in His eyes. If only some are selected, then all are not worthy. And how could we ever know who is chosen and who is not? How can we know if we are one of the lucky few? The power of doubt and the schemes of the adversary will use this to wreak havoc on weary souls even if they believe in Jesus.

But there is another way to understand this verse, a way that reveals beauty. To capture this different understanding, there are a couple of translation issues, punctuation, and word meanings to consider, and a few observations that may aid our understanding.

Here is another option:

> Just as He chose us in Him, before the foundation of the world, **to be** holy and blameless before Him **in love, having pre-appointed** us to the plan of adoption as sons through Jesus Christ to Himself, according to the kind intention of His will. (Ephesians 1:4-5, my translation from the Greek.)

The first observation to consider is that this verse says God "chose us in Him … to be holy and blameless before Him in love." This verse does not say God chose us *to be in Him* as if He chooses those who are out of Him and places them in Him. The only way to *get* in Him is to *believe* in Him. We are in Him, and He chooses us for the purpose Paul specifically identifies. We are chosen in Him *to be*[109] holy and blameless before Him in love. Being holy and blameless in love is a description of God's desired experience for us—our walk, not our standing or position. We are chosen for a task. The purpose for which we are chosen in Him is to be holy and blameless in love in our walk with Him.

Secondly, the word "chosen" (*eklegō*) is a word that was commonly used to refer to the process of selecting:

> People to perform a certain task, or administer a certain office … and the selection of individuals … for a particularly difficult or glorious mission … it is the election itself which makes it possible for him to take up his function and which at the same time lays an obligation upon him.[110]

The idea behind the word *chosen* has more to do with the task to which a person is appointed or called to perform (*eklegō* is a compound of *ek*: out, from + *legō*: to speak or call).

The task to which we have been chosen or appointed is to be holy and blameless before Him in love. Or, as Paul describes elsewhere: our "calling with which we have been called" (Ephesians 4:1). This is a calling to walk in a manner worthy of the One who called us. Our calling is to walk in love: love God and others. Harold Hoehner, in his commentary on Ephesians, thinks the emphasis on the subject of love is actually love for others. He writes: "the predominant use … is between humans."[111]

In short, we are to live a life of love. Love is what we have been chosen for and called to.

Love is our glorious mission. Love is the task at hand. To live love, we seek the good for others because in so doing, we communicate to them—and all watching—that they are worthy of love. This is God's high calling.

This predetermined plan involves a new status that is explained in Ephesians 1:5: "He predestined us to adoption as sons through Jesus Christ to Himself."

With some minor punctuation changes (a comma where there usually is a period) and changing the translation of a word—in particular, a misleading word in English—the verse makes sense. The word translated "predestine" in the original Greek (*proorizō*) does not mean what the English word *predestine* implies. This Greek word has nothing to do with our destiny. And it especially has nothing to do with our eternal destiny. A better translation of *proorizō* is "to pre-appoint."

Dr. Gordon Olson observed: "Since the idea of 'destiny' is not at all present ... the translation 'to predestinate' is totally erroneous."[112]

The most common way in which this Greek word was used was for the pre-appointment of a person to an office or task. This goes right along with everything we have seen thus far about God's choosing. God chooses some to certain venues of service. The service to which some are pre-appointed comes with obligations to fulfill.

Many think adoption as sons describes the process of someone coming to God or Jesus Christ. It does not. Adoption describes our status once we are in Christ. This status or standing (with all its privileges) is what we are pre-appointed to. The object of pre-appointment is not the person but the plan and privilege; He chose us, having pre-appointed us to *uiothesia*.[113] It is not the *who* which is pre-appointed but the *what* one is pre-appointed for.

We have been pre-appointed for a *standing as sons* who have the opportunity to inherit the riches of the Father. This status gives us the right to participate in the *"patria potestas* (power of the father) in the next generation,"[114] but this newfound status comes with certain obligations that must be met before the rights and riches of the Father can be awarded to the sons. God did not predetermine *who* would believe in Christ; He predetermined *the plan* for those who would believe in Christ. This forward-focusing, obligation-loaded understanding of choosing for service with the privilege of great reward is exactly the same idea behind other verses such as Romans 8:28:

> And we know that God causes all things to work together for good to those who love God, to those who are called according to *His* purpose. For those whom He foreknew, He also predestined to become conformed to the image of His Son, so that He would be the firstborn among many brethren; and these whom He predestined, these He also called; and these whom He called, He also justified; and these whom He justified, He also glorified.

These verses come in the context of a vibrant and victorious walk with God. It takes place while we look forward to our future hope of glory (Romans 8:24-25). We are called according to His purpose, which is explained by His foreknowledge and pre-appointment—Greek: *proorizō* (same word as Ephesians 1:5)—which comes with the obligation "to be conformed to the image of His Son."

Loving God and fulfilling our calling according to His purpose will result in being conformed to the image of His Son, even if that might come by way of suffering (Romans 8:17-18). This process of transformation is the means through which we will be glorified with Him (Romans 8:17, 30). The difficulty of persevering through trials, always loving God, and staying true to our calling, will not compare "with the glory that is to be revealed to us" (Romans 8:18). We will realize the fullness of what is promised to us in the coming glory as we fulfill the obligation of our calling and appointment.

In all these passages, God is not picking and choosing who gets to go to heaven and who must go to hell. God does not do that. God is not selecting some to love like a schoolyard child playing duck, duck, goose. God loves all and considers all to be worthy of love. God wants all men to be saved and to come to a full knowledge of the truth (1 Timothy 2:4). That is the truth. Anything else is a lie. Clear statements like "desires all men to be saved" cannot be true if God chooses who will be saved and who will not. God does not believe in the unconditional election of man's systems of theology. God doesn't work by the concept of unconditional election that man has formulated in his systematic theologies.

If you believe in Jesus Christ, you are in Him and have been selected to be His servant. You have a calling from God. That calling is to be holy and blameless before Him in love. That calling has the potential for great reward and riches. And when you live, love, and shed God's light, you stir up love and jealousy that God will use to bring people out of the bushes and back to the Garden.

God chooses you to look forward, not backward.

There is a very good reason car designers and manufacturers design the rearview mirror to be relatively small in proportion to the windshield. Designers know that when we drive our car, most of the driving time is spent going forward. This fact makes looking forward of greater importance. Also, when we drive forward, we are going at higher rates of speed and have more to consider. When we back up, we are usually going much slower, taking our time, and narrowing our focus.

I know that may sound overly simplistic, but it is profoundly true. There are some drivers who like to spend more time looking in their rearview mirror (they are more concerned with what people are doing behind them or they are grooming themselves). As a result, they are not moving forward very efficiently or safely. Hopefully, they are at least in the right-hand lane. Windshields are large and rearview mirrors are small because we need to be looking forward. We need to focus upon what is in front of us more than what lies behind.

The same is true in life. Living free of shame is about knowing where you stand and about looking forward. If God picks and chooses whom He loves, and if He does not love all, then we can never be absolutely sure about where we stand. At least we can't be sure in this lifetime. That insecurity and lack of a sense of our worth and significance are hazards on the road of life. That is no way to live. If a child grows up in a home that lacks acceptance and unconditional love, more often than not that child will grow into an adult who lacks confidence to boldly live and love. If we make performance of our children a necessary way for them to feel secure or assured of our love, they will be looking back (introspection or retrospection) more than looking forward.

We have misunderstood key verses and turned them into rearview mirrors—looking back to see if we are among the elect—when, in reality, these verses are windshields through which we ought to see where we are going: to the calling and riches God has chosen us for. If we are honest, the picture of God that is conjured up with so many of these misunderstandings is not pretty. In fact, the image of God we are creating is beastly. As we listen and read with fresh perspectives, we see the beauty emerge from the beast.

There are many men and women—smart, well-intentioned men and women—who hold different views and would disagree with the perspective shared here. These folks are often adamant about their version of the truth. How is one to decide? Be still. Listen. Weigh and consider. Pray. Look for what makes the best sense. Look for what fits the whole story. Look for continuity. Look and listen for what is consistent with what you see revealed in Jesus, for "truth is in Jesus" (Ephesians 4:21).

Millard Erickson wrote that "more jokes have been made about this doctrine (predestination) than about all other Christian doctrines combined."[115]

The doctrine of predestination and unconditional election is a joke. And not a funny one.

I'm certainly not laughing.

Hawaiian Guy

Someone once wrote that the two most important days of a person's life are these: the day they were born and the day they figure out why.

Every single human being ever born matters to God and has incredible intrinsic and essential worth. That you can be sure of. But what about the second most important day?

Why do you exist? Who are you and why are you here?

- To be a banker?
- To be a doctor?
- To be a teacher?
- To be a preacher?

What you do for employment is not why you exist.

How you balance books, fix broken bones, instruct others, or deliver a sermon is not why you are here. There is something bigger. There has to be something bigger. What we do as a career is not the sum total of why we are here. Maybe this chapter will help you discover the second most important day of your life: the day you figure out why you were born.

- We are chosen of God to bear His light to the world.
- We are saints, set apart.
- We are chosen to serve and let the light shine so the whole world might see how wonderful and loving our God is.
- We are chosen to beam intrinsic worth. This is the same responsibility Israel had as God's chosen nation, and it is the

same responsibility they will take up again in the future. But now it is ours.

- We are the chosen to serve, to shed light.
- We are saints, set apart. The only reason anything is ever set apart is for a purpose. This is why you were born. This is why you exist. The important question is: *What do you want?*

We can know who we are and why we were born. We can know our purpose is far greater than we ever imagined. We know that lawyer, banker, teacher, salesman, or preacher is what we *do,* not who we *are,* or why we are here. At some point we must decide what we want.

I once heard someone pray, "Let there be more light than heat."[116] Do you want more light than heat? Do you want your life to be about something that dispels darkness or burns people?

When we accept that our lives have far greater significance than the jobs we do, the paychecks we deposit, the widgets we make, the houses we build, or the vacations we enjoy, we are on our way to making Jesus active in every facet of our lives. Jesus said, "Let your light shine before men in such a way that they may see your good works, and glorify your Father who is in heaven" (Matthew 5:16). Let Him shine through you.

When I think about this, I cannot help but think about Chuck, the trash man. Chuck is a Hawaiian guy. Please understand, no job is beneath us, and I do not intend to belittle Chuck's job as a city trash collector, but I doubt many parents dream that refuse collection will top their children's list of dream jobs.

Chuck is a bright, intelligent, well-spoken man (still a hint of *Olelo Hawaii* accent). At one time, he drove a city truck and collected trash. He could have done other things, I am sure, but Chuck was not simply a trash collector. He had a greater understanding of the reason for his existence. Chuck used his trash route to shed light and love. His job may have been ordinary, yet he did it extraordinarily. On any given day, you might have found Chuck out of the truck carrying on a conversation, helping someone, or being a shoulder to cry on.

The apostle Paul wrote that he was willing to "be expended for … souls" (2 Corinthians 12:15) and that he poured out his life as a "drink offering" (Philippians 2:17; 2 Timothy 4:6). Paul did that. Chuck poured out more than he picked up. We can do the same. It is what we have been chosen for.

---

106 Oscar Wilde, *The Picture of Dorian Gray.*

107 Peter Loader, *Such a Shame - A Consideration of Shame and Shaming Mechanisms in Families* (1998).

108 I say "not all bad" because obviously love within the body of Christ should not be jealous (1 Corinthians 13:4).

109 present infinitive of *eimi* the verb "to be" can indicate the goal or purpose.

110 Colin Brown, *Theological Dictionary of the New Testament*, I, p536.

111 Harold Hoehner, *Ephesians*, pp.181-182.

112 Gordon Olson, *Getting the Gospel Right*, p.267.

113 I have written more extensively on this subject in *Majestic Destiny: Kingdom Hope is Rising*, chapter 13: *Welcome to the Family*, pp.200-217.

114 Harold Hoehner, *Ephesians*, p.196.

115 Millard Erickson, *Christian Theology*, p.907.

116 Possibly may have been Ravi Zacharias who prayed this.

Chapter 12
Avoiding Religious Schizophrenia

If we don't change our direction we
will end up where we are headed.
~ Chinese Proverb

A number of years ago, when my youngest son was two or three years old, we were visiting a fish hatchery on the Metolius River. It was a cool spring day in Oregon with a whisper of snow still on the ground. After taking in the fish at the hatchery, we all ventured out to walk the trail along the river. My youngest has always been quite an adventurous and active spirit. This day was no exception. The wilderness was his playground. When it was time to turn back, I told him to return to me so we could head back to the car. He had his own agenda—which he would not abandon—so he ignored my instructions. I took the opportunity as a teachable moment.

Our group was on the way back to our car. My son, however, continued farther and farther down the trail away from the car and me. His journey went on for five or so minutes as I followed closely behind, ducking behind trees so he wouldn't see me. I watched and waited to see what he would do. He kept wandering, obviously distracted and amazed at all his eyes could take in, and at the joy of a walk in the woods. He may have been momentarily enjoying his independence. Finally, he stopped. He turned completely around and then made one more circle. That's when reality sunk in: he was all alone. He burst into tears ... big crocodile-type tears. His independence and confidence were fully drained from him. Once he looked back and saw that none had gone with him, he lost all confidence. He felt abandoned, alone, and scared. I swooped in, grabbed him up in my arms, and hugged him.

After the tears stopped, I explained to him the importance of listening and obeying, and how easy it is to get lost in the woods. I told him I loved his adventurous spirit and sense of wonder. I also told him—and I have many times since—that I would always be there for him, and he never had to worry or wonder about that.

He learned some important lessons that day.

He hasn't gotten lost in the woods since.

But he hasn't lost his sense of adventure and wonder. And, most importantly, he has grown into a fine young man whom I believe knows without a shadow of a doubt that Dad is always there for him, accepts him no matter what, and always loves him.

This may be one of the single most important goals of parenting: to ensure our children know we love them, accept them, and are there for them no matter what. Parents want their children to soar, to be adventuresome, and to wonder. And we want them to do so with total confidence, knowing that, regardless of what happens, they can always turn and find support, acceptance, advice, and love from Mom and Dad. Parents should never want their children to be preoccupied with worry, doubt, or concern as to whether or not Mom and Dad will be there for them. Growing up with fear of rejection or abandonment is at the heart and essence of shame-based families.

Children who grow up without that solid foundation will typically end up working frantically to please, perform, and be perfect in order to earn or maintain acceptability and love. Because they don't feel love, they learn to adapt to love as a "moving target,"[117] dependent on their present perseverance or performance. Kids need environments that fuel their sense of wonder. The only way for them to be creative and adventurous is to know they belong and are accepted for who they are—not what they do or don't do. They can be preoccupied with the adventure, not with whether or not they belong or have support and acceptance. Acceptance is not something we earn. To think that way will only make us preoccupied with the wrong thing.

Parenting 101, right? Of course.

Would it not seem completely counterintuitive to assume God would treat His children in the opposite way? If it is a true principle of healthy parenting, then our heavenly Father makes the mold and writes the book on this stuff. God would never want His kids living in fear of rejection or abandonment. He does not want us to be preoccupied with whether or not we are acceptable based on capability or accomplishments.

Most people fear abandonment by God because they have been taught they lack intrinsic value and worth, because they are damaged, dead, and damned. These unfortunate folks actually believe they deserve to be abandoned or rejected since not only can they do no good, they *are* no good. Others fear abandonment because they don't understand the character of God. This is why we love verses like, "I will never leave you nor forsake you" (Hebrews 13:5).

That gets at the very core of what we need most: security, surety, and stability. We need not be preoccupied with whether or not we are loved by God, accepted by Him, and wondering if He is always there for us. As our newly-shaped perspective of God continues to emerge and grow and we become more confident in dispelling errant beliefs about Him, we should grow more and more confident and assured of our capability and connection. We ought to learn that we don't need to look back to see if God is there. He is *always* there.

Unfortunately, that is not how most Christians live.

Many Christians have a very unhealthy preoccupation with self. They are always looking and checking, gauging and judging, constantly trying to figure out if they are doing enough. This is because someone taught them that is how they can know whether or not they are one of the chosen of God, one of His elect. The Puritans wrestled incessantly with this problem.[118] We should not be preoccupied with self. We ought to be preoccupied with Christ. This is the reason the author of Hebrews tells us to "run with endurance the race that is set before us, fixing our eyes on Jesus, the author and perfector of faith ..." (Hebrews 12:1-2).

Looking over our shoulder makes us wonder, *If I do this, will I still be accepted? If I don't do this, will I continue to be loved?* What is worse is that many people live as if what they do proves whether or not they ever were loved and accepted to begin with. Imagine the problems with this line of thinking: fear and shame.

We are going somewhere, but the only way to get there is to look forward and go full steam ahead.

Where Are We Going?

In the movie *Planes, Trains, and Automobiles*, an unlikely pair, Del Griffith and Neal Page, played by John Candy and Steve Martin, are dubiously paired up with each other along a traveling adventure gone wrong—Murphy's-Law-kind-of wrong. In one scene, another pair of travelers, driving their own car, roll down their windows and start yelling at Del and Neal, "You're going the wrong way!"

Those other travelers knew Del and Neal were driving on the wrong side of the highway against the flow of traffic. Del and Neal were oblivious since they were not paying attention as they entered the highway, but they were definitely going the wrong direction. Del, being completely unaware of his driving blunder and making no sense of the warning from the concerned travelers, responds to their frantic message, "How do they know where we're going?" Neal shrugs it off saying, "Yes. How do they know where we're going?"

Well, as luck would have it—in Del and Neal's case *bad* luck—they were going in the right direction, but doing so the wrong way.

Evaluating your surroundings is important as long as you know what to look for and where you are going. Direction matters.

Knowing how to get there is important too.

Don't fall into the trap of thinking you must look at your life to determine to whom you belong. God loves you and accepts you without reference to what you do. He promised He would never leave you or forsake you no matter what you do or don't do. Don't get preoccupied with self. Many people say the only way you can know you belong to God—that you are one of the elect, one of those whom He has chosen—is by looking at your life. Yikes! This is the hazard of the errant belief of unconditional election. You have nothing to prove.

It is exactly this kind of thinking that drives people to a frenetic, performance-based existence that leads to what can only accurately be described as religious schizophrenia. It is utterly destructive and defeating to think your worth and value as a human being are connected to your doing. Shame will drive you to the religious nuthouse with the label *schizophrenic*. This is not healthy.

If you have been on this merry-go-round, I have one question for you: *Aren't you tired?*

Jeff VanVonderen observed that "... most of the literature, seminars, sermons, and counseling available to Christians have one thing in common: they give already-tired people something more *to do*, which is exactly what they do not need."[119] Doing more is not how you find rest and worth.

This reminds me of a young lady named Susan who was raised in a home where acceptance was strictly based on performance. For the most part, Susan is a well-adjusted adult, but even as an adult woman she easily drifts into periods of being so driven to stay busy, she does not allow herself any down time where things are just quiet. She realizes when she gets in this place—so busy there is no space in her life where she can hear her thoughts—it is not her happy place. It truly is a life of schizophrenic busyness. There are moments when those who know her best see it when *it* starts to ... when *she* starts to unravel. When that happens, it is messy.

Setting the Record Straight

As we have seen throughout this book, the election of God is about His temporal purposes to establish His kingdom upon this earth through a people of His own possession, in order that all the families of the earth may be blessed. But at some point, a friend or acquaintance will come along and hit you with a verse like 2 Peter 1:10 which reads:

> Therefore, brethren, be all the more diligent to make certain about His calling and choosing you; for as long as you practice these things you will never stumble.

Your well-intentioned friend may use this verse to get you to try harder, prove you are one of God's chosen (through your trying harder), or introspect and analyze your efforts to know you are in God's graces. Many people think this verse is teaching us to get busy so we can make God's call and choice of us a permanent experience. What the heck does that even mean?

Is there a better way to understand this verse?

Yes, there is. This verse (and the calling and choosing) has nothing to do with heaven or hell or where you stand positionally or relationally with God. This verse is not teaching you to be introspective to determine if you are connected to God. The calling and choosing are toward something in the future, and how you live today makes something certain about that future potential. This verse is actually teaching us to look forward to what we are called and chosen for. It does not teach us to look at our present or past to decide what God may or may not have done in the past. This verse is not telling us to objectively or subjectively look for confirmation of God's predestination of us as the elect. Ironically,[120] John Calvin himself said:

> If you contemplate yourself, that is sure damnation ... by good works, nothing will be more uncertain or more feeble ... (works) judged of themselves, by their imperfections they will no less declare God's wrath than by their incomplete purity they testify to His benevolence ...when the Christian looks at himself he can only have grounds for anxiety, indeed despair.[121]

Calvin was correct. Looking to ourselves will only lead to anxiety, despair, and uncertainty, making us feel feebler. Sounds like the makings of a perfect definition of religious schizophrenia. Schizophrenia is a mental disorder characterized by disintegration of thought processes and emotional responsiveness. It most commonly manifests itself in auditory hallucinations, paranoid or bizarre delusions, or disorganized speech and thinking. It is accompanied by significant social or occupational dysfunction. Seeking assurance of one's standing, value, and worth through a contemplation of religious efforts leads to religious schizophrenia. See what another pastor and author has to say about this verse:

> When Peter says, "Be zealous to confirm your call and election," he means that our lack of diligence in Christian graces may be a sign that we were never called and are not among the elect.[122]

Schizo!

When we fall into the trap of thinking our lack or bounty (of performance) determines or reveals whether we belong to God or not, we can become paranoid and prone to delusions. When we think our works have some bearing on whether God loves us, we become very prone to perfectionism and performance, trying desperately to make sure He is pleased with us.

What a shame. And a sham.

God has promised great riches that He wants to abundantly supply to you upon "entrance into the eternal kingdom of our Lord and Savior Jesus Christ" (2 Peter 1:11). This is the reason we are to be diligent, because being diligent is how we make certain, or guarantee (*bebaios* means *secure, sure, or guarantee*) our rich and lavish entrance into the kingdom when it comes. This is what we have been chosen for and called to. Only I can *make*[123] certain that guarantee for myself by being diligent. I am not proving to myself or to anyone else that I belong to God. Such an idea will only lead me directly to religious schizophrenia.

If a person, for example, was very intentional about securing a satisfactory nest egg for his retirement, he might choose to do so by putting money aside in a 401K or an IRA. The diligent will make certain (or guarantee) he will have a sufficient amount in his retirement by investing regularly. By being faithful to make regular deposits, he will guarantee the outcome. For those who misunderstand this election and calling and make it something with reference to our eternal salvation or standing with God, it would be like saying the way for a future retiree to make certain about his calling and having been chosen, is to call ETRADE every day to check his account, just to make sure he still has an account.

Laying Up Treasure

Living this verse out in our own realities is a "bulwark against failing."[124] If people are "looking for and hastening the coming of the day of God," they will be people of "holy conduct and godliness" and "found by Him in peace, spotless and blameless" (2 Peter 3:11-14). People who make their call and election sure are those who do not stumble. Having met the obligation, they will be assured/guaranteed a rich welcome.

The calling and election is to a greater and richer end: to be "fellow heirs with Christ" (Romans 8:17) and to "reign with Him" (2 Timothy 2:12). The way to make that certain is to "have these qualities and increasing" so as "to practice these things so as to never stumble" (2 Peter 1:8-10).

It's been said that "there is nothing certain except death and taxes." I disagree. You can be certain that if you fulfill the virtuous living called for in 2 Peter 1:5-7, you will never stumble or fall from your steadfastness. Therefore, you can be absolutely assured your entrance into the eternal kingdom of our Lord and Savior Jesus Christ will be ABUNDANTLY supplied to you—if you invest in His 401K plan today and do so faithfully.

The proper way to understand calling and election is all about direction. God doesn't want us looking back or inward to ascertain that we belong to Him. God wants us to *know* we belong to Him so we can look forward, move forward, venture out, wonder, and invest in our future.

Shame works exactly the opposite. Shame wants us to be insecure. Shame wants us to be introspective. As Sandra D. Wilson writes, "Shame puts us eternally on trial, and the verdict is always *guilty.*"[125]

It is a slippery slope to religious schizophrenia.

Know the direction you should be looking and heading, and keep moving forward.

---

117 Brennan Manning, *All is Grace*, p.57.

118 see John Owens volume 3, pp 45-47; 226-28.

119 Jeff VanVonderen, *Tired of Trying to Measure Up*, pp.11-12.

120 I say "ironically" because Calvin would also refer to this very verse in complete contradiction to his point. As would many "Calvinist" after him, and Puritans, etc.

121 R.T. Kendal, quoting John Calvin Institutes III.ii.24; xiv.19; Commentary 1 Cor. 1:9.

122 John Piper, sermon: *Confirm Your Election* (May 2, 1982).

123 The verb "make" is in the middle voice which means "the subject performs or experiences the action expressed by the verb ... the subject acts with 'vested interest'" (Dan Wallace, *Greek Grammar Beyond the Basics*, pp.414-415).

124 Jodi Dillow, *Reign of the Servant Kings*, p295.

125 Sandra D. Wilson, *Released from Shame*, p.91.

Chapter 13
Avoiding the Land of Ism

*Understanding the difference between healthy striving and perfectionism
is critical to laying down the shield and picking up your life.*
~ Brené Brown[126]

In the book *The Cure*,[127] authors John S. Lynch, Bruce McNicol, and Bill Thrall discuss the two roads Christians choose to walk. The first road is called the "Road of Pleasing God," and it leads to the "Room of Good Intentions." This road and this room are full of rules and laws, standards and objectives, most of them too hard to reach and impossible to reconcile with the God set before us in the Bible. Nonetheless, they are an essential part of succeeding along this first path.

The second, and better, road is the "Road of Trusting God" which leads to the "Room of Grace." On this road and in this room, you get to be the real you (no need for masks). Performance-based entrance and acceptance are foreign ideas. Formulas for godliness are left behind. There is kindness, warmth, love, and, of course, grace. Here, God meets you where you are, wraps His arms around you, and walks with you the whole way and the whole time, no matter what may come (or what mistakes you make). This road—trusting God—and this room are vibrant, authentic, loving, deeply satisfying, and full of laughter and freedom.

But there's another path the authors discuss that some of us choose to take. It usually happens after we've struggled up the Road of Pleasing God and found ourselves to be disheartened after years in the Room of Good Intentions. Some of us leave that room and simply find a soft bed of grass to lie down on. We get off the road, don't choose another, and sit out the rest of life. The issues were too confusing, and trying to make sense of it all became overwhelming. We redefined man's laws as God's and found keeping up with them all wasn't worth the pain.

Jeff VanVonderen catches the essence of this downward spiral when he writes:

> After realizing the sense of shame I'd had for so long, the second thing I saw on the night my life began to change was this: All my life—and mostly without even knowing it—I'd been trying to measure up to the standards of other people, including my own family and my Christian environment. Even tougher, I'd been trying to live up to the standards of an utterly holy God who, I was so often reminded, could not tolerate even one whiff of sin. Living with that continuous sense of shame, I'd entered into a process that involved three steps: trying, trying harder, and trying my hardest. Did I say three steps? Actually, there were four: I gave up—or at least I switched the standards by which I was trying to measure myself. True, the alcohol and drugs could have killed me physically, but to be honest, even though I had been a Christian, I was already nearly dead inside.[128]

This is a sad indicator of the trouble shame causes. What is even sadder is that this is anything but an isolated event or phenomenon.

Most researchers, bloggers, authors, psychologists, and preachers who write or talk about shame all seem to agree that shame leads to very destructive habits of perfectionism, performance-driven mindsets, legalism, judgmentalism, and hypocritical living—the essence of religion gone wrong. Shame is the feeling that one is unworthy of belonging and love. Shame says you will never measure up, you don't deserve the ground you occupy, and no matter how hard you try, you will never do enough, and it will never be good enough.

Why do people who grow up in shame-based families tend to be driven by performance, perfectionism, and legalism? Because this is how people seeking value and worth fit in or hide.

Let's return to Mike once again. His dad told him in no uncertain terms that he was worthless. No matter how hard Mike tried, whatever he did was never enough or good enough. He felt like a mistake and a disappointment. On top of that, his dad told him he would never amount to anything. Once Mike was out of the house and on his own, what do you think he did? He got busy trying to make something of himself. He got busy working long hours, scheming and striving to make himself a success. The problem was, of course, he was doing it for all the wrong reasons. In the end, the success was empty, and his dad never acknowledged his son's accomplishments anyway. What happened next to Mike may surprise you.

Mike went to church and found Jesus.

Unfortunately, the version of God he was taught was not a whole lot different than his earthly father. He still felt lower than pond scum, not sure if he was a mistake or one of the chosen. He still had something to prove. He still had value and worth to earn. Once again, he got busy because he was continuing to allow—albeit unknowingly—shame to be his guide to life.

This is the way shame operates. Shame likes to be our tour guide to life. It is willing to take control and direct our paths if we let it. But the paths it leads us down, the destinations it takes us to, are not good, healthy, or safe. Shame leads us down the Path of Pleasing God to the Room of Good Intentions, a room full of rules, laws, and standards to meet. It gladly guides us to legalism, perfectionism, performancism, judgmentalism, Pharasaicalism, and isolationism.

The church is a perfect incubator and creator for all of the above. It is a secretly seductive place for shame-laden people. The church is a place to *belong*. The vision statement of the church I pastor is: *A place to begin, belong, and become*. Belonging is a good thing. But since the church—generally speaking—has such skewed perspectives of God and man's worth, belonging comes with expectations, rules, and order. The church generally is very structured about what you can do and what you cannot do, what you can believe and what you cannot believe. It is a very easy place to come, fit in, and get with the program, so to speak. It is a great place for the shamed to come and perform while doing "the Lord's work."

Unfortunately, when people who are battered by shame come to the church and "get with the program," the church thinks it hit the new member jackpot or lottery. They will appreciate everything you are doing (attending, tithing, serving). You will learn the unwritten rules and be a model citizen while others will pat you on the back and give you the praise you so long for ... until you stop *doing*. You stop because you get tired. It is called burnout because you have been doing the right things for the wrong reasons and from the wrong source. The church will use you up and spit you out. Gone are the days when the church existed and ministry happened organically as people grew and were led by God to serve in the area of their giftedness and passion. The church has become so program-driven that it is like a vacuum, sucking warm bodies into "ministry opportunities." If you get sucked in for the wrong reasons—or work from the wrong source—you will eventually want to give up. There is no air in a vacuum.

This is a vicious cycle.

Shoulds

What the church needs is for you to be healthy and whole, following God's leading in your life because you already know you are worthy and loved. Then you are not *doing* church; you are *being* church. We need more people being church rather than doing church. What you do and who you are in the church are no different than the person you are outside its four walls because you *are* the church. The church needs the authentic you. But with all these errant beliefs about God, the church is wrongly driven to *should* all over people.[129]

- If you are a Christian, you *should* read your Bible every day.
- If you are a Christian, you *should* pray faithfully and without ceasing.
- If you are a Christian, you *should* serve in the church's ministry.
- If you are a Christian, you *should* tithe every month.
- If you are a serious follower of Jesus, you *should* …
- If you loved God with a crazy love, you *should* …
- If you are radical for God, you *should* sell your big house, drive an old beater car, etc., etc., *ad naseaum* so that you could give more, do more, and go more. Because you *should* …

What we really need is to correct our errant beliefs about God and stop with all the "ratchet Christianity." We need to stop *shouldin'* all over each other.

It is messy. It is destructive. It causes more hurt.

The God I see in the Bible—and in Jesus—is not judgmental, demanding, duplicitous, unfair, and selective like we have been taught. The answer to shame is never to be better, try harder, do more, discipline yourself more, give more, pray more, or sell more. The answer to shame is rightly understanding God and resting in Him, knowing He understands you and loves you just as you are, for who you are. God is not putting demands on you to perform or be perfect so you are acceptable or loveable. God knows this equation ends disastrously. Doing the right thing for the wrong reasons is legalism.

The late Ray Stedman commented on legalism in a sermon, saying, "I know of no affliction in Christendom which is more widespread and more devastating in its destructiveness than this." Or as Arthur Wallis wrote, "Legalism is Satan's most effective means of infiltrating and undermining the work and witness of the church."[130]

When the church is inherently legalistic, it fosters the monster of shame. There has been more than enough written on the issue of legalism and Pharisaicalism, but what I hope you see here is the way it is connected to shame.

In a Christian context, it suits us to lump such things into one category because they all fit under the same umbrella.

Legalism is ...

First of all, *legalism is impersonal.* We are not wired to engage with rules; we are wired to engage with God and others. But most importantly, legalism robs us of a chance to be who God made us. Legalism is all about the rules, order, and demands. It is not about you or me, or me together with you; it is about the rule and the law. Legalism kills any personality and personal expression.

When I must toe the line, I don't leave space to be the real me—the mistake-making, out-of-the-box, creative, perfectly imperfect me. Personality brings life to a community of people, which is why God has made each one of us unique. It is why ministry in the church can be an expression of the "manifold grace of God" (1 Peter 4:10). The Spirit of God desires to energize each person to use his/her God-given gifts and talents in a way that no one else, of a different personality, could. There is no sense of personhood or personal worth in a life of impersonal rule-following, performance-oriented, perfectionistic, Pharisaical religion. It is highly doubtful that God would ever want a mass of religious drones following the rules and order without the energy of His Spirit and ours (John 4:23-24).

Second, and closely connected to the first, *legalism is lonely*. Legalism produces isolation. While you may have some who are joining you in "the fight," those who do so are with you only as long as you remain on the team and keep up the show. Living a legalistic life will only make you more judgmental and demanding of others. We will complain because 20 percent do 80 percent of the work. We will be exasperated because everyone else is not as faithful as we are. We will develop critical spirits that quickly and easily spot everything everyone else is doing wrong—and we feel it is our job to point it out. As Brené Brown writes:

> Finding someone to put down, judge, or criticize becomes a way to get out of the web or call attention away from our box. If you're doing worse than I am at something, I think, my chances of surviving are better.[131]

The legalist has been taught that they are only valuable if they do the right things. Failure is not an option, so when others don't comply, they are ready to use the club on others that was used on them.

Most others will be driven away by your moral and spiritual superiority or judgmental and condemning spirit—all of which come with the package deal of legalism. Shel Silverstein wrote a cute little poem titled *My Rules* that captures this sentiment perfectly. It goes like this:

> *If you want to marry me, here's what you'll have to do:*
> *You must learn how to make a perfect chicken-dumpling stew.*
> *And you must sew my holey socks,*
> *And soothe my troubled mind,*
> *And develop the knack for scratching my back,*
> *And keep my shoes spotlessly shined.*
> *And while I rest you must rake up the leaves,*

And when it is hailing and snowing
You must shovel the walk ... and be still when I talk,
And—hey—where are you going?[132]

When rules and rule-keeping become the focus, people eventually come to the conclusion that life is better off lived separate from legalists. Rules and relationship are difficult to harmonize. If rules are necessary in order for relationship, then when those rules are broken, so goes the relationship. Rules are *never* more important than people. God gives laws because He knows when we trust and follow Him, we avoid things that hurt us and cause pain. When we trust His guidance, we live at peak performance. God's ways are good for us, but they are never more important than we are.

This is why Jesus ran into so much trouble with the Pharisees over the Sabbath. The Pharisees had lost sight of the fact that "the Sabbath was made for man, and not man for the Sabbath" (Mark 2:27). Everything that can be done for God is for our good and must be done with relationship as the priority. This is why when Jesus taught the disciples the right way to live, He warned about people who would gravitate to the doing without the knowing of relationship. Jesus said, "Many will say to Me on that day, 'Lord, Lord, did we not prophesy in Your name, and in Your name cast out demons, and in Your name perform many miracles?' And then I will declare to them, 'I never knew you; DEPART FROM ME, YOU WHO PRACTICE LAWLESSNESS" (Matthew 7:22-23).

The knowledge Jesus said was lacking was a deeper, more intensive knowing of experience. These folks were busy working for Jesus, but it was all about busyness. Jesus puts a higher premium on relationship than following rules and being busy for God.

Legalism is pharisaical and hypocritical.

Nobody is perfect at obeying the rules, especially when doing it for the wrong reasons. If you are doing it to suck life out of others by trying to appear worthy, you will only come up more empty of life. Religious people are really good at learning the rules and putting on a face they think others expect from them. Our peak performance is in the life of Jesus Christ. It is not in changing me, but exchanging my life for His. I am imperfect. He is perfect. In Him I can be perfectly imperfect or imperfectly perfect but, most importantly, I can be me.

I visited a church in Houston, Texas, a few years back and the motto or vision statement of the church was: *No Perfect People Allowed*. When Christ prayed what we call His "high priestly prayer" (John 16-17), He asked the Father to make us one, not perfect in our law-keeping or rule-observance. The only way for us to dwell together in unity is to do so with grace and love as we are imperfectly perfect or perfectly imperfect.

When we finally come to grips with the fact that God is good— all the time—and that He considers us worthy of love right where we are—and most importantly for *who* we are—we can stop seeking validation from others and stop trying to earn a sense of worth. God wants us to walk in His presence, not live according to a list of things to do. I love what VanVonderen wrote: "The problem is not the length of the list, but that there is a list at all."[133]

Legalists would never memorize verses like "mercy triumphs over judgment" (James 2:13). Legalists are not kind. The legalist usually tries to force everyone by guilt and shame to do what is expected ... what *they* expect.

If shame has guided you to a life of legalism, you are not being the real you. Shame changes people, so they believe "it is dangerous to let the real mistake-making you show."

> So we fashion disguises, masks of perfection. These masks are extremely cumbersome and ill-fitting. We get exhausted holding them in place. They constrict and chafe since they weren't designed to fit real, imperfect people like you and me.[134]

Stop pretending. It is okay to be imperfect. It is okay to be broken. Casting Crowns has a powerful song that captures the very essence of what I believe marriage ought to be, and the basic idea applies to all relationships. The title of the song is "Broken Together."[135] If you haven't heard it, I urge you to. The heart of the song is a plea. It depicts a marriage on the brink of collapse. The dreams of the couple have turned sour as romanticized expectations and imperfect people collided. As the title suggests, the dire request of the heartbroken spouse is to live this imperfect life as imperfect people, side by side, "Broken Together," allowing grace to entwine the hearts and mend the pain. It is a cry to be loved for who they are.

It must be safe to make mistakes. It must be safe to be yourself.

This is the kind of community that is well-suited to shine the light of God's grace and love to the whole world. If we cannot be loving and gracious with our own, how can we ever expect to be effective as ambassadors of reconciliation (2 Corinthians 5:20)? We are reconciling others to God, not to Christianity, especially some version or order of Christianity we have been taught and have accepted.

A.J. Swoboda writes about how we need to separate love and grace from agreement, as if agreement means we cannot love and support others with whom we disagree. He writes:

> God gives me food, water, and air every day, and I'm pretty sure he disagrees with me 99 percent of the time. Love and grace don't require agreement. It requires a blanket. It requires love.[136]

Finally, legalism is fatalistic. Legalism will kill off any of the *you* that remains. If I do the right thing for the wrong reason, especially to be validated and considered worthy of belonging and love, the pitfalls are unavoidable. I will never be confident that I have done enough. I will never be subjectively sure that what I have done is good enough. And, eventually, people won't pat me on the back. They may fail to appreciate me. I will disappoint myself, and I will be disappointed by others. And where will all that leave me? Probably worse than when I began. But here is the biggest problem with legalism and why it is fatalistic. Legalism sucks the personal intimacy out of the relationship we can have with God. At the end of that short walk is total despair. This is where people tend to give up, even on God, and quit altogether.

Lost and Found

The bright side is that when we break free of the rules, order, and demands, and begin to see God for who He really is—and we grasp our intrinsic worth that is absolute and not conditioned upon anything we do or don't do—we are really ready to live freely, openly, and authentically.

What kind of God are you beginning to see? What image of God is emerging from your freshly-gained perspective? Maybe you still have some deconstructing to do before construction begins.

Just like the lost sheep, the lost coin, and the lost son, God seeks that which is lost because everything—and everyone—matters immensely to Him. God will leave ninety-nine sheep to find the one lost. He will sweep the house if one of the ten coins comes up missing. And He will throw a party and cling lovingly to the neck of the prodigal son who returns home. God values all sheep, all His coins, and all His sons. There is "joy in the presence of angels" when what is lost is found (Luke 15:7, 10, 32). The only reason this could be true is because everyone matters to God.

God loves all His wee little children. The story of Zaccheus is a wonderful illustration of how we tend towards being legalistic, judgmental, and performance-based, yet how wonderfully loving and good God is.

Jesus said, "Zacchaeus, come down immediately" (Luke 19:5 NIV). How do you read those words? Maybe you prefer to sing them:

> Zacchaeus was a wee little man, a wee little man was he.
> He climbed up in a sycamore tree for the Lord he wanted to see.
> And as the Savior passed that way He looked up in that tree.
> And He said, "Zacchaeus, you come down from there![137]

If you grew up in a fundamental or traditional church, I'll bet you can't sing that song without wagging your index finger at the wee little man when you sing that last line: "Zacchaeus, you come down from there!" The legalist mindset is that Zacchaeus was not a good man, and God was ticked off at Him for collecting taxes and climbing trees. He was outside the box of the rules and order of what the religious society of his day considered worthy and acceptable. So Jesus was wagging His finger at the wee little man when He told him to come down. Right? Is that really who you think God is? Do you think God is the finger-wagging God you have been taught? The finger-wagging god is a shame-shaped deity that does not fit what we know about God.

God is not standing in disapproval. Our worth and value to God is not based on what we do or what we don't do, so He will not sit at the base of the tree and wag His finger at us in shame. If you want an accurate picture of God, then go back to Jesus. Take a look at a clue in the story of Jesus and Zacchaeus that maybe, just maybe, we have been allowing shame to guide us. Read two verses together, Luke 19:5-6:

> When Jesus came to the place, He looked up and said to him, "Zacchaeus, hurry, come down, for today I must stay at your house." And he [Zacchaeus] hurried and came down, and received Him gladly (i.e., rejoicing).

What is missing? Finger-wagging.

What is more obvious from the passage? Zacchaeus was excited at the presence and prospect of being with Jesus. He hurried down, received Jesus (literally, "welcomed Him"), and if that was not enough, he did it all while REJOICING.

Rejoicing. Zacchaeus had joy, not shame. He did not want to disappear off the face of the earth. He knew in that very moment he mattered to God. Zacchaeus did not feel judged or condemned.

My guess is—and it is purely a guess—Jesus was not wagging His finger; He was opening His arms. Jesus was good at that.

Jesus did not tell Zacchaeus to get his life right, stop doing such and such, quit his job, and sell his camel (to buy a donkey) so he would be acceptable to God. There is no judgment. No condemnation. No demands. There is love. Acceptance. Value.

Jesus' invitation and acceptance of Zacchaeus, a real sinner and chief tax-gatherer caused quite a stir from the religious folk, however (Luke 19:2, 7). This is what we expect from people who put performance over personal worth. Maybe those Pharisaical, legalistic, performance-driven, shame-based religionists wrote the nursery song with the wagging finger.

Hmmm?

It has been said that in the beginning, God created man in His own image and ever since we have been trying to return the favor.[138] The image of God we create, even with the best of intentions, is not a pretty picture. A.J. Swoboda writes that you know "you have created God in your own image when God hates everyone that you hate … (or) you have created God in your own image when God approves of everything you do."[139]

Who is the God you worship? Is He like what you have been taught and indoctrinated to believe or think, or is He more like Jesus?

What we think God does or is, translates directly into what we do to others and ourselves. If God is a shame-shaped deity, we will become little shame-shaped deities too. If we think God values obedience and observance of the rules more than He values us for who we are apart from what we do, that is where we will dwell and where we will drag others to join us.

Enough is Enough

Why do we shame others? According to Jeff VanVonderen:

> Shame is often used by people as a means of placing themselves over others. When I give you a message that you are bad or defective, I am placing myself in the position of being more valuable, or more powerful, and the judge of your value as a person.[140]

Legalism and shame-based living deteriorate into competitive living … finding someone who is inferior so I can feel better about myself.

The disciples fell into the trap on more than one occasion. Jesus' response is not only surprising but very telling. Jesus said, "Unless you are converted and become like children, you will not enter the kingdom of heaven. Whoever then humbles himself as this child, he is the greatest in the kingdom of heaven" (Matthew 18:3-4). Jesus followers are to turn and be like children. This begs the question: what are children like? In shame-based families, parents usually demand and expect their children to act like adults, but children are not adults, they are kids. And apparently there is something to the way a child goes about life that is admirable and should not be lost even when we become adults. Here is my take on what is unique and admirable in children that Jesus says we all need to turn back to.

Children are humble. A child does not try to be someone he is not. He is okay messing up and usually has very short memories when people wrong him or when he does wrong. Children don't have highly sophisticated and developed filters. They are much more naturally authentic. They say what is on their mind and ask a lot of questions. Children are innocently and wonderfully whole and sufficient even while being utterly dependent. They are like that until we demand they act like adults—or we damage them and make them fit the mold we think is right. Before we mess them up, children start out thinking they are enough.

Brené Brown writes:

> Believing that you're enough is what gives you the courage to be authentic, vulnerable, and imperfect. When we don't have that, we shape-shift and turn into chameleons; we hustle for the worthiness we already possess.[141]

No matter how much you do or how well you do it is not the way to establish that you are enough. You are enough because God says you are enough. Your intrinsic worth, value, and lovability are not based on what you do.

Enough is enough.

Jesus said, Enough! Be like a child.

Shame twists all of this and makes ugly out of beauty.

If we think performance is the pathway to significance and belonging, we are on the slippery slope to legalism. That slide ends in even more emptiness and usually leads to more bitterness, anger, depression, or worse. We need to accept that God said enough is enough.

Shame on Jesus

Legalism has adverse effects on us. And there is one more seriously bad twist. Legalism brings shame to Jesus Christ. That is right. When we fall back into performing to gain worth, we are, in essence, saying what Jesus did was not enough.

When this happens, we are bringing shame to the person and work of Jesus Christ. Let me explain.

The author of the New Testament book of Hebrews realized this sort of thing was happening in his day, and he wrote to correct this devastating and destructive practice. Within the group of Hebrew Christians he was writing to, there was a group of people resorting back to a legalistic, performance-based practice of an old religious system (Judaism) and trying to force others into doing the same. Shame loves to control others.

But in doing this, they were implying the sacrifice of Jesus on the cross was insufficient for them. It was a disgraceful practice and totally unnecessary. That is why the author wrote, "It is impossible to renew them again to repentance, since {or while} they again crucify to themselves the Son of God, and put Him to open shame" (Hebrews 6:6).

Living in legalism when Christ died once for all to free us and communicate worth to us was to bring shame upon Christ. Little hope existed for fellowship until they put a stop to this shameful activity. Their thinking about God was wrong. Going back to a performance-based religious system of sacrifices was to put Christ back on the cross, metaphorically speaking. It basically communicated to others that Jesus' death was not sufficient for all sin and His resurrection was not sufficient for life. This is a wrong perspective of God and what was meant by the statement "and put Him to open shame." Either Jesus' death was sufficient or it wasn't, but because He said it was when He said "It is finished!" (tetelesttai) then to reason and live in a way contrary was shameful, for the people *and* for Christ.

When Jesus said "It is finished!" it meant enough is enough (John 19:30).

When we believe the lie and live like our acceptability and worth are contingent upon obedience or performance, we are saying God is not enough. We are saying the work of the cross was not enough. We are saying Jesus is a liar.

There are three stages in the work of God: impossible, difficult, done![142]

"If trying hard were the key to the victorious Christian life, you'd probably be in the Hall of Fame by now. You don't need to learn more ways to try hard. Christians need to learn how to rest."[143]

Jesus said to those of His day who were guided by shame, "Come to Me all who are weary and heavy-laden, and I will give you rest" (Matthew 11:28).

Our peak performance is to rest in Jesus. He is our life.

God wants our hearts, not our heartless performance (Isaiah 1). "It was for freedom that Christ set us free; therefore, keep standing firm and do not be subject again to a yoke of slavery" (Galatians 5:1). "Now the Lord is the Spirit, and where the Spirit of the Lord is, there is liberty {freedom}" (2 Corinthians 3:17). That word for freedom means no bounds or restraints (of legalistic religion).

Don't go backward. Go forward.

Follow the path of freedom. Follow the Lord.

126 Brené Brown, *The Gifts of Imperfection*.

127 Bill Thrall, John Lynch, Bruce McNicol, *The Cure: What If God Isn't Who You Think He Is and Neither Are You?* (2011).

128 Jeff VanVonderen, *Tired of Trying to Measure Up*, p.20.

129 Thanks to Jerry Price for that nugget!

130 Arthur Wallis, *Radical Christian*, p. 155.

131 Brené Brown, *Daring Greatly*, p.98.

132 Shel Silverstein, *Where the Sidewalk Ends*, p.74.

133 Jeff VanVonderen, *Tired of Trying to Measure Up*, p.39.

134 Sandra Wilson, *Released From Shame*, pp.94-95.

135 Casting Crowns, *Thrive*, Provident Label Group, 2014.

136 A.J. Swoboda, *Messy*, pp. 84-85.

137 Quoted from www.makingmusicfun.net.

138 Quote is attributed to Voltaire, see www.goodreads.com.

139 A.J. Swoboda, *Messy*.

140 Jeff VanVonderen, *Families Where Grace is in Place*, p.29.

141 http://www.oprah.com/spirit/Life-Lessons-We-All-Need-to-Learn-Brené-Brown.

142 James Hudson Taylor, quoted from www.goodreads.com.

143 Jeff VanVonderen, *Tired of Trying to Measure Up*, p.11.

Chapter 14
Hiding or Abiding/Bushes or Boldness

The biggest enemy to compassion is shame.
You were born to show
fierce love. Let nothing stand
in your way.
~ Danny Silk[144]

The following are definitions of *hiding* in Merriam Webster's Dictionary: *To put or keep out of sight; to prevent disclosure of; conceal; to cut off from sight; to cover up.*

Hiding is what I do:
- When I am afraid.
- When I feel rejected.

Hiding is where I go:
- When I am alone.
- When I feel shame.

There are many reasons, trappings, and enticements of life that will try to seduce us into hiding, as if life was not hard enough on its own. Life continues on every day, and the *stuff* always rolls downhill. If you are not "in it," then brace yourself; it is coming.

We grow up, get responsible, and go to work in our respective careers. Some of us get married, raise kids, and engage in community of some sort (faith-based, hobby, pleasure) or civil activities, among other things. At every turn, there is real and present danger that may cause shame to you or those you love, or aggravate old scars left by shame. Marriages fail, children rebel, and jobs disappoint. Life is messy. Relationships are messy. Everything is messy. Shame loves messiness.

Shame uses the messes of life to destroy relationships. The majority of marriages end up in divorce because one partner or the other just could not do it anymore. They could never do enough or be good enough. *They* were not enough. If those marriages don't end bitterly, they go on day after day enduring in bitterness and isolation. This is a painful method of hiding because it is a slow grind. The worst kind of loneliness is when people are alone together. It looks something like this: Working, running about from one activity/responsibility to the other, coming home, minimal conversation or interest, knocking back a few glasses of wine (or worse) to numb oneself and induce sleep so they can manage and muster up the strength and fortitude to get up and do it all over for one more day. Until they don't.

It can be like the young man or woman who feels so alone, unloved, and desperate that even mustering the strength to try another day is vanishing like sand in an hourglass right before their very eyes. Lives are extinguished by suicide on an all-too-frequent basis because people can no longer be alone and unloved. These are just a few examples of hiding. Divorce is a form of hiding. Addiction is a form of hiding. Suicide is the most severe and final form of hiding.

Hiding is what we do to cope. Hiding is sourced in evil. It is one of the fruits of the tree of the knowledge of evil. Hiding is death. Sometimes it is a slow death. Other times it is quick.

Lewis Smedes writes: "We are ready for grace when we are bone tired of our struggle to be worthy and acceptable."[145] We need to get mad and take a stand. We need to get fed up with hiding. Are you tired enough? Are you ready for something different? Something better?

When Adam and Eve went into hiding, God called out and asked, *Where are you? What have you done? Who told you that you were naked?* When it was time for God to address the serpent, there were no questions. God said to the serpent, "Because you have done this, CURSED are you." No questions, just a sentence: cursed.

The Devil wants us afraid, shamed, and hiding. God is about destroying the works of the Devil (1 John 3:8). God is our Advocate, one called alongside to help (John 14:16; 1 John 2:1). The devil is the destroyer (Revelation 9:11) who roams about the earth "seeking someone to devour" (1 Peter 5:8). This enemy is the "god of this world {age}" (i.e., the system of the world and the way most people think) (2 Corinthians 4:4) and seeks to blind our minds. He wants us in darkness … in hiding. The enemy wants us to live a living death. If that sounds like an oxymoron, it is. Death is no way to live. Hiding is no way to live.

God knows exactly where we are today. God asks:

- *Where are you?*
- *What have you done?*
- *Who told you that you are naked (or that naked is bad)?*

Why does God ask? Why does He call out to us?

He beckons and invites us out of the bushes, out of hiding, to enjoy life. He *is* life. The life He has for us is called eternal life. Eternal life is abundant life. Eternal life is God's life. The only answer and solution to hiding and death is LIFE.

Don't listen to the god of this age. Life cannot be found apart from the one true God. It has been tried. Seeking life in our jobs, hobbies, accomplishments, or in other people has proven futile, empty, and frustrating. Solomon's wisdom rings truer today than ever:

> Vanity of vanities! All is vanity. All things are wearisome; man is not able to tell it. The eye is not satisfied with seeing, nor is the ear filled with hearing. That which has been is that which will be, and that which has been done is that which will be done. So, there is nothing new under the sun. (Ecclesiastes 1:2, 8-9)

Stop listening to the voice of reason of this age. There is nothing new under the sun. It has been tried and tried, and all who travel this path come up wanting. As Solomon wrote elsewhere, "God made men upright, but they have sought many devices" (Ecclesiastes 7:29). Life is not found in devices of this age. Many of these *things* can be enjoyed since God "richly supplies us with all good things to enjoy" (1 Timothy 6:17), but they are not a source of life, worth, and significance. There are many ways we think are right, but the end of them is death (Proverbs 14:12).

God is the creator and sustainer of life. God *is* life. We all long for meaning, significance, and love that can only be found in God. The only way out of death is life. Jesus said, "He who hears My word, and believes Him who sent Me, has eternal life, and does not come into judgment, but has passed out of death into life" (John 5:24). This is a transition from death to life that is for today—not when our time on earth ends. Today!

So many think Jesus came to give us a safe place to land when we die (life in eternity), but this skips over the best part: eternal life *today*. I like the way the late Ray Stedman said it:

> Not life in quantity, although it does include that—it is endless life—but primarily life in quality. Life abundant, life exciting. Life adventurous, full, meaningful, relevant. Life that is lived to the fullest, that is God's gift to man.[146]

Jesus' way of putting it is shorter and better: "I came that they may have life and have it abundantly" (John 10:10). Eternal life. Life exciting. Life abundant. Life adventurous, full, meaningful, relevant. Life to the fullest.

Eternal life is not affected by time (i.e., change) and the messiness of life. No matter how chaotic[147] and messy things get, eternal life does not change because it is the very life of God. God is the same "yesterday and today and forever" (Hebrews 13:8). This is eternal life, and it is for today.

To survive and thrive, we must come out of hiding. We are not made to live alone, afraid, despairing, and in darkness. We are created for life. Eternal life. God's life.

Eternal life is to be lived in intimate experience.

Jesus defined eternal life for us when He said, "This is eternal life, that they may know You, the only true God, and Jesus Christ whom You have sent" (John 17:3). Knowing God is eternal life. Knowing God is how we experience and share in His abundant life. This *knowing* is more than data or information in our heads. Although it is certainly that, it is an intensively deeper experience of Him.

This is where faith comes in. Not a onetime moment of faith, but a constant and continual walk of faith. Faith is the way we draw out the life of Jesus in us which is present through the power and presence of the Holy Spirit. Jesus said when the Spirit comes, "He will glorify Me, for He will take of Mine, and will disclose it to you" (John 16:14).

This is why Paul could later write, "I have been crucified with Christ; and it is no longer I who live, but Christ lives in me; and the life which I now live in the flesh I live by faith in the Son of God who loved me and gave Himself up for me" (Galatians 2:20). The life we live—life out of hiding, out of the bushes—is lived by faith. Faith is how the branches appropriate the life of the Vine. Apart from Him we can do nothing (John 15:5). "And without faith it is impossible to please Him" (Hebrews 11:6).

Another important word used as a synonym for faith: *abide*.

Abiding is living. It is communing with Jesus. This is how Jesus lived in communion with the Father (John 14:10) and how He told His disciples that productive life was lived (John 15:4).

Abiding is making our home in God and God making His in us. Bushes are not your home. God is home. Abide in Him and He in you.

Axioms of Abiding

We all need a little help sometimes, so to begin or maintain abiding in God, let's identify a few important and foundational principles of abiding.

Abiding begins with thinking rightly about God. One of the Ten Commandments says not to have any graven images/idols because even an erroneous understanding of God works adversely to abiding in His presence. If I don't know who He truly is, I will be more likely to hide than abide. If I have errant beliefs, I have a wrong version of God and not the true God; I have an idol. Greg Boyd states it rather plainly: "At the root of all that is wrong with humans is a false and ugly mental image of God."[148] This must be why the apostle John concluded his first epistle, an epistle written to foster fellowship (abiding) with God, with these words: "Little children, guard yourselves from idols" (1 John 5:21). An idol can be any perversion of God or a creation of God as we imagine. Abiding in Him means we must *know* Him.

You may have identified a problem and some conflicting ideas. You may be stuck between the system of theology you were taught and the hope of a new way to understand God. Go back to the Scriptures and look at the clear statements about who God is. Then be still and know that He is God. Abide.

Jesus said, "I and the Father are one" (John 10:30). Jesus said, "I am the true vine, and My Father is the vinedresser" (John 15:1). Jesus said, "I am the bread of life" (John 6:35).

The apostle John wrote, "God *is* light and in Him there is no darkness at all" (1 John 1:5).

John also wrote, "God *is* love" (1 John 4:8, 16) and that Jesus "*is* the propitiation for our sins, and not for ours only but also for those of the whole world" (1 John 2:2). These are not statements about what God does, but who God *is*. (Italics mine.)

Start here. Abide in light and love … satisfied.

Abiding expects right thinking about man. Since abiding can only take place outside of hiding, we must be confident that it is safe to come out and be seen. You are not lower than pond scum. You are not utterly damaged, dead, or damned.

You are not unlovable or incapable. Just because it is by grace and we may not *deserve* it does not mean you are not worthy of it. You long for love and belonging, and you are worthy of both. Brené Brown talks and writes about how the path away from shame is "vulnerability." Brown defines vulnerability this way: "We must dare to show up and let ourselves be seen. This is vulnerability. This is daring greatly."[149] Dare greatly to come out of the bushes. It is safe for you—the real you—to come out. In Brown's thoughts, she calls this wholehearted living which she defines this way:

> Wholehearted living is about engaging in our lives from a place of worthiness. It means cultivating courage, compassion, and connection to wake up in the morning and think, "No matter what gets done and how much is left undone, I am enough." It's going to bed at night thinking, "Yes, I am imperfect and vulnerable and sometimes afraid, but that doesn't change the truth that I am also brave and worthy of love and belonging.[150]

You are enough. You are not perfect. You have weaknesses (we all do), but you are worthy. Come out!

Abiding is living loved. My sister has this very postscript—Live Loved—on every email she sends out. This is very simply, but wonderfully, profound. We must live from a solid sense of being loved. Abiding in God is an experience where Jesus dwells:

> ... in your hearts through faith, that you, being rooted and grounded in love, may be able to comprehend with all the saints what is the breadth and length and height and depth, and to know the love of Christ which surpasses knowledge, that you may be filled up to all the fullness of God. (Ephesians 3:17-19)

To know the love of Christ, we must be "rooted and grounded in love." Love is the foundation for abiding. Jesus said, "Just as the Father has loved Me, I have also loved you; abide in My love" (John 15:9). The apostle John wrote, "God is love, and the one who abides in love abides in God, and God abides in him" (1 John 4:16).

Knowing you're loved is the foundation for all victorious Christian living. Let me repeat that. *Knowing you are loved is the foundation.*

Jesus said the two greatest commandments are to "LOVE THE LORD YOUR GOD ... and YOUR NEIGHBOR *AS YOURSELF*" (Matthew 22:37-39). The standard of loving your neighbor is doing so "as you love yourself." We must know we are loved to live loved.

How can we know we are loved—or lovable?

It is very simple. "We know love by this, that He laid down His life for us" (1 John 3:16). The word translated as *know* is the Greek word *ginōskō* which, unlike its counterpart *oida*, refers to a knowledge much deeper, intensive, and experiential than mere intellectual insight. This word is a stative verb which means it describes a *state* of being, not an action sort of verb like, "I *hit* the ball." This knowing is more than data processed in the mind. It is an experience of being loved through an unparalleled expression of love: "Greater love has no one than this, that one lay down His life for His friends" (John 15:13). Our absolute intrinsic worth and lovability comes from God who "first loved us" (1 John 4:10).

Live loved. When you live loved, you love living.

Abiding is for the real you. We are all broken, weak, and sinful people. We do not need to get our act together and fix all our problems in order to come out of hiding and begin abiding. We come as we are. God loved us "while we were yet sinners" (Romans 5:8). There is no application or qualification process in order to abide. God is for us, not against us.

To know and be known is our greatest joy and also our greatest fear.[151] There is a great level of uncertainty and risk in relationships. People will not always receive or perceive us the way we think or intend. This is completely out of our control. If we allow others to dictate or determine our authenticity, we give them control they don't deserve. Most of us live in shame as we "lug around inside a dead weight of not-good-enoughness."[152] Being the real you is an essential step in abiding in Him and abiding in His love.

If you never live authentically, showing the real you, you will never truly appreciate or understand the depths of God's love. If you learn to put on a face or perform according to expectation, you are not being the real you and will never know for sure if the real you is loved. You are only truly loved to the degree you are fully known. I think it was Dallas Willard who used to say, "When you are abiding in His life, you are not concerned with outcomes." Be free of the anxiety and worry of the outcome of being you. Be you. Abide.

Even if you mess up or are weak, still be you.

We are so impatient and ungracious with each other, but as Paul found, "I am well content with weakness ... for when I am weak, then I am strong" (2 Corinthians 12:10). How could Paul get to this place of being content? Because God told him, "My grace is sufficient for you, for power is perfected in weakness" (2 Corinthians 12:8). Our personal pathway to this confidence is the same as it was for Paul. Abide.

God is for us.

When we "walk in the light," God is at work—behind the scenes if you will—when we are yet unaware, to cleanse us from all sin by the blood of Jesus (1 John 1:7). Because God is light, and in Him there is no darkness. God is at work to dispel and eliminate darkness in us so we can share deeply in His presence.

A little side note is needed here. While God cleanses, we never reach a state of sinless perfection as if we are "without sin" (1 John 1:8a). To think otherwise is pure deception and "the truth is not in us" (1 John 1:8b). Don't ever be like the Pharisee who said, "God, I thank

You that I am not like other people: swindlers, unjust, adulterers, or even like this tax collector" (Luke 18:11). Rather, humbly abide like the tax collector who prayed, "God, be merciful to me, the sinner" (Luke 18:13).

Sometimes God cleanses, and other times He convicts.

God convicts us to reveal certain specific sins which, for our own growth and well-being, we must own up to. God brings conviction so we might experience guilt—very different than shame—and be driven back to Him for love, grace, mercy, and forgiveness. We respond to this conviction by agreeing with Him (i.e., confessing) those sins. Confession might be verbalized in words, expressed in thought, or it might just be an alignment of your heart with His on the matter. It is between you and Him. When we align our minds and hearts with His on these issues and confess our sins, "He is faithful and righteous to forgive us our sins and to cleanse us from all unrighteousness" (1 John 1:9). Forgiveness (lit, "send away from"[153]) is exactly what we need when we sin and feel guilty. We need to experience a clean conscience. We need to know that forgiveness exists from God so we can also forgive ourselves and not let it turn into shame.

To deny His conviction is to attempt to invalidate Him and His truth (1 John 1:10). This is what shame does. If we are invalidated, we invalidate the invalidator, making His invalidation of us invalid. God convicts; He does not shame.

Confession is good for the soul.

Remember, we have an Advocate who can sympathize with us, to help us in these times of weakness (1 John 2:1; Hebrews 4:15-16).

Jesus is rightly qualified, for He is propitiation. Jesus is rightly situated at the right hand of the throne of God.

This is what God does for all who abide.

Abiding quiets many voices. You are already likely aware there are many voices that try to straighten us out or condemn us along our journey. As we abide in Him, we will learn to listen to what others have to say, but will not necessarily take what they have to say as being the definitive source of truth about us.

Oftentimes, the voice is none other than our very own. We can be our own worst enemy. Abiding in Him silences or tunes out those many voices. John writes, "If our hearts condemn us, we know that God is greater than our hearts, and He knows everything" (1 John 3:20 NIV). Shame exaggerates faults, and we are very adept at such exaggeration. Sandra D. Wilson writes:

> Self-shaming is expressed by inner-commentaries on our consistent failures … Self-shaming administers punishment for the crime of imperfection, and the sentence is either the death penalty or life imprisonment.[154]

Shame exaggerates faults, but God is greater than our hearts. When we abide in Him, we find rest, knowing He is in charge of convicting us of sin. Since He knows all and knows best, He is trustworthy. We are not the best judge of our own hearts.

I treasure what Paul wrote:

> But to me it is a very small thing that I may be examined by you, or by any human court; in fact, I do not even examine myself. For I am conscious of nothing against myself, yet I am not by this acquitted; but the one who examines me is the Lord. (1 Corinthians 4:3-4)

It is not a big deal if others examine us. We should not even examine ourselves in this way. God examines us. If God reveals something to us as we abide in Him, then we can look at it and deal with it appropriately. Abiding quiets many judgmental and critical voices.

One voice is enough. Listen to Him.

Abiding is a journey, not a destination. We are all in process. At present, we must abide in Him and He in us. There will be a time when we will abide together. As the Scripture says, "Beloved, now we are children of God, and it has not appeared as yet what we will be. We know that when He appears, we will be like Him, because we will see Him just as He is" (1 John 3:2). It will be messy at times; that is life. It will be unpredictable. It will be imperfect. But it is a journey, not a destination. We will be messy at times. We are in process.

Living is learning. School is not out. We always have room to grow and go.

We are all in the same boat. We are all perfectly imperfect, or imperfectly perfect. We need to lighten up on ourselves and each other.

Abiding prepares us for the destination. We are told to "abide in Him, so that when He appears, we may have confidence and not shrink away from Him in shame at His coming" (1 John 2:28). Abiding now leads to confidence (lit, "all speech") later when He appears.

How we respond to Him when we see Him face-to-face will be directly dependent upon how much we have come to know Him by abiding now. Shame is a natural experience when you meet God face-to-face, and you are not sure who He is or how He might act. This is not saying God is ashamed of us, but our lack of knowledge of Him will cause us to hide. It will be a small and final victory for our adversary.

Abiding in this way is transforming, not conforming. John wrote, "And everyone who has this hope fixed on Him purifies himself, just as He is pure" (1 John 3:3). Consider the words of Paul: "But we all, with unveiled face, beholding as in a mirror the glory of the Lord, are being transformed into the same image from glory to glory, just as from the Lord, the Spirit" (2 Corinthians 3:18).

Abiding is experiential, not existential. The shame equation is: one wrong act equals one bad person.[155] God forgive us for this judgmental and condemning spirit. I figure it is best to start there. Abiding is about knowing God experientially.

It is totally illogical and false to think you can fix worth or eternal standing on the basis of what someone is doing, or not doing. Reread and rethink verses like 1 John 2:3: "By this we *know* that we have come to *know* Him, if we keep His commandments." Dive into the Greek with me for just a moment. Breathe in deeply and dive. Both words translated *know* are the Greek word *ginōskō*, which, as I previously mentioned, is a stative verb—a verb which describes a state of being/experience. The second of the two *ginōskō* verbs is a perfect tense stative verb, which emphasizes the present results in order to intensify the meaning: thus a deeper state of *knowing*.[156] Why is this important? Because this verse says we can know by experience what we are in the process of knowing deeply, namely that we are knowing Him experientially if we keep (treasure) His commandments. This describes experience, not eternal standing or intrinsic identity. Experiential knowledge of God is evidential. To have a vibrant, abiding experience, I must always maintain the distinction between who I am and what I do.

I am a human *being*, not a human *doing*. I am not defined by my actions, even if those actions may characterize me at times. My actions, or lack thereof, may tell me something about the nature of my experience, but they do not tell me about my essence or worth. If I look to my actions to ascertain my intrinsic worth … well, you see the problem here, right?

Abiding is about experience.

Abiding eliminates fear and hiding. Fear is crippling and has adverse effects to abiding. Dr. Tim Jennings writes: "Fear and love are inversely proportional."[157]   The more fear one experiences, the less love one feels or experiences at that same moment. The opposite is inversely true: the more love one feels, the less fear one will experience.

God's love and fear do not coexist together.

Abiding in God is abiding in His love and allowing His love to abide in you. God's love is perfect and "there is no fear in love; but perfect love casts out fear" (1 John 4:18a). The reason perfect loves acts this way toward fear is stated in the next part of the verse: "… because fear involves punishment, and the one who fears is not perfected in love" (1 John 4:18b).

Most English translations say "fear involves punishment," but there may be a better way to understand this so it is clearer. I like how the Message Bible puts this one: "Fear is crippling." The word translated as "punishment" was used in its verb form to "cut off, lop, trim, hence prune," and has the idea of crippling or restraining something to create a greater effect. It is the idea of stunting something to cause more growth. This same word (*kolasin*) is used in the Septuagint to translate Hebrew words (*kashal, mikshal*) which mean "stumbling block, obstacle" or "to stumble, stagger, to fail or be feeble." This verse is not saying fear is because we are going to get punished, and that is why love casts it out. Fear is crippling. Fear is an obstacle to love. Fear hinders love. Fear restrains us from growing in love or being a place where love is completed. Fear stunts our experience of love. Fear is an

DAMN SHAME

obstacle to love. Abiding is living loved, so since fear hinders, it is cast out.

Fear seems reasonable to us, but it is not. It is *false evidence appearing real*. Fear is what causes us to stop abiding and retreat back into hiding. Danny Silk wrote:

> Fear-based reactions to pain are instinctive, which means that they operate at a very different level in your brain than conscious, rational choices. You execute them without thinking. And because they come so naturally, they seem normal.[158]

What we fear most is being rejected and/or not validated as worthy and lovable. Perfect love casts out this fear—utterly and completely. Or, as one author puts it:

> One of the greatest problems facing the human being is doubt. It is a measure of our insecurity. Security is surety. If we are secure, we are sure. If we are insecure, we are unsure. One of our greatest insecurities deals with our worthiness to be loved and our capacity to display love. Inside of us hides something dark, so depraved that we are scared to death someone will discover who we really are and what we are really like. We fear if they did, no one would like us, and no one would love us, precisely because it is this part of our selves we detest, we dislike, and we abhor.[159]

Fear limits us, yet love has no bounds. Fear is an obstacle to love, but perfect love casts out fear. Abiding in love diminishes and dismisses fear.

Abiding is dying, not trying. Abiding in God's presence is not a constant pressure on our wills to do more and try harder. Abiding is not trying at all. It is about *dying*. Jesus said on more than one occasion that if a man wants to save his life, he must lose it (Matthew 10:39; Mark 8:35; Luke 9:24; 17:33; John 12:25). Eternal life is not found by trying harder to do life on our own. Trying is not the pathway to victorious Christian living; it is dying to self and living to Christ. The life we live in Him, by abiding in Him, is lived by faith in Him that "we might live through Him" (1 John 4:9).

Faith taps into His life so that He expresses Himself in and through us to do what we could not otherwise do. When we stop trying and are satisfied with dying, "His commandments are not burdensome" (1 John 5:3).

There is nothing heavy about something if you don't have to lift it.

If it were about trying, or trying harder (and harder and harder), then His commands would become heavy and weigh us down. Jesus said, "Come to Me all who are weary and heavy-laden, and I will give you rest ... for My yoke is easy, and My burden is light" (Matthew 11:28, 30). Dying and abiding is the victorious Christian life because "whatever is born of God overcomes the world" (1 John 5:4). It is not *what* you know but *who* you know, the old saying goes. It is not what you know, but *Whom* you are knowing.

Abide in Him. He will do all the heavy lifting.

Abiding produces joy. Even in the midst of a trial or hardship of life, we can gain a perspective from God that can help us "consider it all joy" when we "encounter various trials, knowing that the testing of your (our) faith produces endurance" (James 1:2-3). That word for endurance literally means "remain under." When we have this perspective—and we abide in Him and He in us—we can remain under the trials and still have joy.

When Jesus taught the disciples about abiding in Him, He said, "These things I have spoken to you so that My joy may be in you, and that your joy may be made full" (John 15:11).

Abiding in Christ brings joy.

Abiding has Spirit guiding. When Jesus told the disciples He was leaving, and where He was going, they could not follow at that time. He made a promise to send the Holy Spirit to them to be their Helper. One way the Spirit would help, said Jesus: "He will teach you all things, and bring to your remembrance all that I said to you" (John 14:26).

And He reminded them soon after that "...when He, the Spirit of Truth, comes, He will guide you into all the truth; for He will not speak on His own initiative, but whatever He hears, He will speak." (John 16:13).

The apostle John would later write the same thing in his epistle on having fellowship with God when he wrote, "But you have an anointing from the Holy One, and you all know ... the anointing which you received from Him abides in you, and you have no need for anyone to teach you; but as His anointing teaches you about all things, and is true and is not a lie, and just as it has taught you, you abide in Him" (1 John 2:20, 27).

The Spirit of God teaches as we abide in Him.

We abide in Him, not in theological systems or doctrines of men. It is relational, not institutional or traditional. He will teach; we must abide.

Without abiding in Him, we are like the natural man Paul described in the letter to the church at Corinth when he wrote, "But a natural man does not accept the things of the Spirit of God, for they are foolishness to him; and he cannot understand them, because they are spiritually appraised. But he who is spiritual appraises all things." (1 Corinthians 2:14-15). If we don't abide, we don't have a sensitivity to His Spirit's guiding; we are fleshly, soulish, and we will not welcome the things He wants to teach us.

With the confidence of our Teacher, we can stop believing every spirit, but "test the spirits to see whether they are from God" (1 John 4:1). We should test everything we read and hear. Everything and everyone. You don't have to stay stuck in the mess and tangled web of beliefs you are in. You may be fearful or doubt your ability to know what is from God and what is from man. Psalm 46:10 (NIV) says, "Be still, and know that I am God." Abide and let the Spirit guide and teach you.

And finally ...

Abiding is Living Love. Not only is abiding living loved, abiding is also living love. As we abide, we are conduits for God's love to reach its goal or completion: others. G.K. Chesterton once wrote, "Let your religion be less of a theory and more of a love affair."[160] This is the very essence of abiding. Abiding is a love affair we have with Jesus and Jesus has with us. It also spills over onto others. Go back and read John 13-14 and the epistle of 1 John. Count how many times the issue of loving others is brought up.

Why is love so important? Because love is what overcomes the world.

The whole world lies in the power of the evil one (1 John 5:19). What is in the world is lust of the eyes, flesh, and the boastful pride of life (1 John 2:16). These are antithetical and adverse to love. The greatest barriers to love are things that reside deeply in us. We need to uncover and overcome all those barriers to love that are built up against loving others. The first is to remember we are loved. Only loved people can love people; hurting people only hurt people. Maybe the barrier that has been built up is your fear of intimacy and having to trust, yet again, at the risk of being hurt. Once again, go back and remember that abiding is living loved.

Sometimes we prop up a barrier because people are so different from us. At times, the more we know, the more reasons we find to resist. Familiarity breeds contempt; the longer you know someone, the more reasons you will find not to love. This is knowledge that becomes a barrier to love. God knows everything about you, and yet He loves you continuously and immeasurably. Abide in His love.

For God's people to open themselves up to be a conduit of love is one way God seeks to complete His love and destroy the works of the Devil.

What does it mean to love?

Love means I communicate intrinsic worth and lovability to people who still remain shackled in shame and hiding in the bushes. Love is God's invitation. God wants us to set up and arrange the meeting. Love changes things. Love transforms. It is about giving life to other people. You and I can only do this from a disposition of love: knowing that we are loved.

Abide in Him. Abide in His love.

The Big Idea

How we think about God affects every area of life. Our thoughts affect our emotions, our minds, and even our bodies. Bad beliefs can mess with our biology. As the proverb aptly states: "For as he thinks within himself {in his heart}, so he is" (Proverbs 23:7).

If your thinking is binding you, blaming you, and shaming you, it is not from God. Change your thoughts. Change your beliefs.

If the God of your doctrine does not match the God you read about in the Bible or see in Jesus, change your theology. If the picture you have of God is not one that leads you to trust and abide in Him, then your thinking is probably not trustworthy. Greg Boyd writes:

> The quality of the relationship can never go beyond the level of trust the relating parties have in each other's character. We cannot be rightly related to God, therefore, except insofar as we embrace a trustworthy picture of Him ... to the extent that our mental picture of God is untrustworthy, we will not rely on Him as our sole source of life ... the root of our alienation from God and our bondage to fallen powers is our untrustworthy and unloving mental pictures of Him.[161]

Is God like so many seem to think, or is He more like what we have discussed in this book? You must decide for yourself. Quiet yourself. Be still and know that He is God. Let His Spirit guide you, remind you, and teach you. If you are listening, you will soon know it is safe to come out of the bushes. If you see Him rightly, you will know it is safe to come out of hiding.

A friend of mine wrote this in an email and I felt it was fitting:

> As I begin to understand more fully the intellectual side of how the process of dealing with pain works in the brain, I find some relief. The self-condemning mantras quiet down a little; the "If you had more faith" and "It's always a matter of choice" voices are leaving me alone more. Those are harsh voices, though they mean well. But it is the growing understanding of my heavenly Father's love for me that truly calms. It is His kindness that leads to repentance ... that draws us closer and allows us to come out of hiding, strip away the coverings we've tried so desperately to cling to, and let Him see the hurt we've concealed. Those critical voices may have some truth in them, but they are often tainted with shame. My Father's voice doesn't have that tone. I'm learning to hear the difference and to discern truth from lie.

There is no need to hide any longer. It is safe. Come and abide in Him. Abide in His love.

We began this journey with Mike, and we shall end with the same. I would be remiss without sharing more of how the rhythm and motion of his story continued.

Mike carried the heavy weight of shame around for years, driving him into hiding many times and seasons of life, in a wide variety of ways. But there was always one bright light in his life: a beacon of hope. This light that never faded was the unconditional love of his mother. Some people are not fortunate enough to have even one parent who loves unconditionally and who is always there to support them no matter what may come. But Mike was lucky that way. He tested his mother's commitment and love multiple times in his rampant, confused, and disillusioned pursuit to please others and find worth and value. This path of performance, people-pleasing, and approval-seeking—which in essence was just shame avoidance—was driven by a desire to prove his father wrong. *He was not a waste of genetic fluid!*

This path led him down many very dark holes. The only way he crawled out of those holes time after time was by following the light of his mom's unconditional love and acceptance. She never approved of the things he did or the choices he made, but she always accepted him, always had room in her heart and love to give. Mike's mom never gave up. The light of her love shined into his darkness.

Mike's mom taught him a lot about God. Without even knowing it, she paved the way for him to find an even stronger sense of worth from his heavenly Father. He discovered that "God is light, and in Him there is no darkness at all" (1 John 1:5). God does not turn His light on and off or dispense it as a commodity. God *is* light. Light dispels darkness. Light draws us out of hiding. Mike was able to grasp this in part because of his mom. He would later have the privilege of leading her to a relationship with the Light of the World.

Ironic? Maybe.

Beautiful? Absolutely!

I wish everyone were as lucky as Mike, but the sad truth is that many are robbed and deprived of this benevolence. It may be harder to grasp the light that God is. It may be harder to feel safe to come out of hiding, to have the darkness dispelled. Regardless of the hardship and deprivation the cruelty of life deals us, the end result can be the same for you as it was for Mike. God waits. God loves. God shines. He is the light to lead us all—for we all have a bit of Mike in us—out of the dark hole that is our shame.

We all wrestle with wanting approval, validation, acceptance, and, most importantly, worth. We will face hard times, harsh people, and we all hurt. Some will experience marriages in which they can never do enough or be enough. Remember, you *are* enough. God says so. Some people will work their whole lives in jobs that seem to go nowhere, never being appreciated or valued and, oftentimes, only hearing criticism and disappointment. You are not your job. You are valuable as a human being. God says so. You begin by being enough and then do your best; you do not do your best to be enough. God says so. In relationship with God, which is based on right thinking about God and ourselves, every morning His mercies are new (Lamentations 3:23). In His presence there is fullness of joy, and in His right hand, eternal pleasures (Psalm 16:11).

Mike recently wrestled through some tough and trying times. He was undergoing some scrutiny and criticism that was very difficult not to take personally. He felt the pull of darkness. *It would be easier to hide,* he thought to himself. Then came the anger and, again, the pull to hide. But then an email, a note of encouragement. The note came from a WWII veteran who reiterated his support and added words of affirmation and consolation that God's hand was upon him and using him. God knows we need a word to edify at times (Ephesians 4:29). The note ended with this postscript: *Damn the torpedoes. Full steam ahead!*

A decision was made at that moment, one Mike knows he will need to make over and over again every time he feels the pull: *Damn the shame. Full steam ahead!*

- Shame is a lie.
- Shame is utterly destructive.
- Shame is a part of the domain of darkness.
- Shame is not from God.

Will you carry the baggage? Will you invite the monster in?

What decision will you make?

---

144 Danny Silk, *Keep Your Love On.*

145 Lewis Smedes, *Shame and Grace*, p.109.

146 Ray Stedman, sermon: *Why Do we Believe?*, July 2, 1967.

147 The 2nd Law of Thermal Dynamics says that as time goes on, entropy increases. Eternal life is not affected by this.

148 Greg Boyd, *The Benefit of Doubt*, p.62.

149 Brené Brown, *Daring Greatly*, p.2.

150 Ibid., p.10.

151 If memory serves correctly I heard this quote from John Ortberg in his recorded presentation at a Dallas Willard symposium.

152 Lewis Smedes, *Shame and Grace*, p.3.

153 Greek: aphiēmi is a compound of 1) apo = "from"; 2) iēmi = "to send."

154 Sandra D. Wilson, *Released from Shame*, pp. 80, 91.

155 Lewis Smedes, *Shame and Grace*, p.17.

156 Dan Wallace, *Greek Grammar Beyond Basics*, "The use of the perfect … focuses on the resultant state. Consequently, stative verbs are especially used in this way. Often the best translation of the intensive perfect is as a present tense."

157 Tim Jennings M.D., *The God Shaped Brain*, p.48.

158 Danny Silk, *Keep Your Love On.*

159 Dave Anderson, *Maximum Joy*, p.175.

160 Quoted from www.goodreads.com.

161 Greg Boyd, *The Benefit of Doubt*, p.235.

For additional resources or to contact the author,
visit www.CurtisHTucker.com.